THE POWER of PRAYER

IN ITS WORKING

THING MOST PEOPLE DO NOT KNOW ABOUT PRAYER

WALTON WEAVER

Copyright © 2024 Walton Weaver.

All rights reserved. No part of this book may be reproduced, stored, or transmitted by any means—whether auditory, graphic, mechanical, or electronic—without written permission of both publisher and author, except in the case of brief excerpts used in critical articles and reviews. Unauthorized reproduction of any part of this work is illegal and is punishable by law.

ISBN: 979-8-89419-352-6 (sc)
ISBN: 979-8-89419-353-3 (hc)
ISBN: 979-8-89419-354-0 (e)

One Galleria Blvd., Suite 1900, Metairie, LA 70001
(504) 702-6708

Table of Contents

1. What Is Prayer? 1
2. Does Prayer Really Work? 13
3. What in the World is God Doing? 25
4. How in the World Is God Doing It? (I) 37
5. How in the World Is God Doing It? (II) 51
6. The Practice of Prayer 67
7. The Qualities of Prayer (I) 79
8. The Qualities of Prayer (II) 89
9. The Conditions of Acceptable Prayer 101
10. The Content of Prayer 115
11. Prayer and Salvation 133
12. Prayer and Confession 149
13. Prayer and the Intercession of Christ............ 165

1

What Is Prayer?

Prayer has been a universal phenomenon as long as man has graced the face of the earth. But Christianity is "the religion of prayer," as Bousset has remarked. Martin Luther expresses this same sentiment about Christianity and prayer in a most remarkable, and yet a quite simple way: "As a shoemaker makes a shoe, and a tailor makes a coat, so ought a Christian to pray. Prayer is the daily business of a Christian."

The subject of prayer is an ever-recurring theme in both the Old and New Testaments, although the subject is more explicitly taught in the New Testament. Ludwig Kohler finds some eighty-five prayers in the Old Testament. About sixty whole psalms and four- teen parts of psalms may be called prayers. Yet, the only explicit instruction regarding prayer in the Old Testament is that which concerns confession of sins (Lev. 5:5; 16:21; 26:40-42).

By way of contrast, in the New Testament not only are Christians explicitly told to confess their sins (Jas. 5:16), but in the Sermon on the Mount alone they are commanded to pray for their enemies (Matt. 5:44); pray, Jesus said, to be heard and seen of God, not men; pray for the kingdom to come, and for daily bread; pray not to be led into temptation; pray that your sins may be forgiven (Matt. 6:5-15).

With so much said in the Bible about prayer, Christians need to know more about the subject, and especially they need to learn to pray more and better. Let us begin this series of studies by attempting to define prayer.

PRAYER AND WORSHIP

Prayer is worship, but not all worship is prayer. Our definition of prayer must not be so limited as to make prayer merely meditation, nor should it be so broad as to make all worship prayer to God. In the Old Testament prayer is often linked with sacrifice (Gen. 12:8; Job 42:8-9; Lev. 5:5-6; 16:21). Sometimes prayer is mentioned alone without any reference to other acts of worship (Gen. 24:12-19; 32:9-12; Num. 14:13-19; Dan. 9:3-19). Prayer then is an act of worship in itself even though it may be offered in connection with other acts of worship.

This same distinction between prayer and other acts of worship is maintained in the New Testament. Paul says, "I will pray with the spirit, and I will pray with the understanding also: I will sing with the spirit, and I will sing with the understanding also" (1 Cor. 14:15). One may pray or give thanks to God either by song or by prayer (v. 17). This shows that each act (singing and praying) is worship unto God, yet they are distinct acts of worship. One may, of course, sing a prayer to God, but the fact remains that singing and praying are distinct acts. When one sings a prayer he is both singing and praying.

DESIRES EXPRESSED TO GOD

Phillip Brooks said, "A prayer in its simplest definition is merely a wish turned heavenward." This definition of prayer is acceptable if by wish we mean the deepest yearnings and desires of the heart, and by turned we mean expressed. Prayer is the desires of the heart expressed unto God. Let us analyze this definition of prayer.

Prayer is DESIRE. Paul says, "Brethren, my heart's desire and prayer to God for Israel is that they might be saved" (Rom. 10:1). He expresses here his intense concern for his own race. In Romans 9:3 he said he could wish that he himself were accursed from Christ for his brethren's sake. His personal bond with the Jews is vividly brought out here. But we are not told that Paul ever expressed this wish to God for the personal sacrifice of himself for the sake of his brethren. He would not pray to God for what was an impossibility.

Prayer is desire EXPRESSED. While Paul would not pray that he might give himself for his brethren, he did both desire and pray for their salvation "my heart's desire **and prayer**...is," Paul says. Prayer in this case was Paul's desire for the salvation of his own people **expressed** to God. While it yet remained simply a sincere desire in his heart it was not prayer to God. When Mary Baker Eaddy, the founder of Christian Science, says, "Desire is prayer...," her definition is inadequate.

We do not read of unspoken prayers in either the Old or New Testaments. Hannah's lips moved as she prayed, but her voice was not heard (1 Sam. 1:13). This does not mean that her prayer was unspoken; it means she spoke in silence to God and could not be heard by others. Paul instructed those who spoke in tongues in assembly to speak in silence to God, if they spoke at all, when there was no interpreter present to give the meaning of their speech (1 Cor. 14:2). Even in silent prayers we are expressing our desires to God.

Prayer is desire expressed TO GOD. The word "prayer" in Philippians 4:6 represents a message that is always addressed to God; "supplication" is a request that may be addressed to either God or man. Prayer is always worship (no matter what form it takes—supplication, thanksgiving, intercession, etc.), and all worship belongs to God. It is for this reason that prayer is distinguished from other speech. This is true because God is omniscient (all-knowing) and because He is omnipotent (all-powerful). This is one reason why the doctrine of the invocation of saints as taught and practiced by some is false. It denies the very meaning of prayer for the Christian. Jesus Himself stated this truth when he said, "Thou shalt worship the Lord thy God, and him only shalt thou serve" (Matt. 4:10). Prayer is to be offered to Deity alone because only Deity is the exclusive object of ALL worship.

TYPES OF PRAYERS

A deeper insight into the meaning of prayer may be gained by making a study of the various terms used in the New Testament to describe prayer. The word "prayer" itself is sometimes used in Scripture in a broad sense to include all the various forms of prayer. At other times it seems to be used with a more restricted meaning. In I Timothy 2:1, Paul mentions supplications, prayers, intercessions and thanksgivings. According to Philippians 4:6 it is by prayers and supplications (both of which are to be accompanied with thanksgiving) that our requests are to be made known to God.

The exact difference between prayer and supplication cannot be known with certainty, but that prayer has a restricted meaning in a passage like I Timothy 2:1 seems to be required by the fact that the word appears in a list with other terms. There may be some merit to the suggestion of some that the word prayer here refers to requests for the fulfillment of needs that are always present (like for wisdom, understanding, greater faith, etc.), whereas supplication refers to requests made in specific situations (like for cure from a certain illness, removal of persecution of a specific type, the salvation of someone in particular, etc.). But whether this difference is to be found in these two words or not, supplication is the stronger of the two words. It is much like the word "beg," taking on the meaning of a very strong request.

The basic idea of the word "intercessions" is "a falling in with," a "meeting with in order to converse freely" (William Hendriksen). But since in this particular context it obviously refers to prayer which is in the interest of others, the English word "intercessions" is most appropriate at this place.

"Thanksgiving" is simply a prayer of gratitude to God. With the psalmist we cry, "Unto thee, O God, do we give thanks" (Ps. 75:1). Paul tells us that "every creature of God is good ... if it be received with thanksgiving" (I Tim. 4:4). From this we learn that even our food is worthy of thanks from a grateful heart which recognizes God as the giver of all good things. Nothing should be taken for granted. There is no heart so mean as the ungrateful heart. As Christians we have so much to be thankful for that we should abound with thanksgiving for all that God has done for us (Col. 2:7).

Prayer is the soul's sincere desire,
Uttered or unexpressed,
The motion of a hidden fire,
That trembles in the breast.

Prayer is the burden of a sigh,
The falling of a tear,
The upward glancing of an eye,
When none but God is near.

Prayer is the simplest form of speech
That infant lips can try,
Prayer the sublimest strains that reach
The Majesty on high.

O thou by whom we come to God,
The life, the truth, the way, -
The path of prayer thyself has trod,
Lord, teach us how to pray!

QUESTIONS FOR JOY AND PROFIT

1. If you are studying this book with others, analyze the poem at the end of the lesson and discuss with them parts you think may give a wrong or inadequate definition of prayer.
2. Select two songs from your songbook that are prayers. Make one a petition and the other a prayer of thanksgiving. Do you sing these as prayers in congregational singing?

3. What is the meaning of Gen. 4:26b, "Then began men to call upon the name of Jehovah"? Does it refer to prayer? If so, did men not pray before this time?
4. If God is the only true object of worship, how explain the following verses? Is. 16:12; 45:20; 44:17; 1 Kgs. 18:26.
5. In what sense might one say that Christianity is "the religion of prayer"?
6. Would you agree or disagree with one writer who said "that prayer is one of those privileges or duties to which one's own nature has prompted him from primeval times"?
7. What is one possible difference between prayer and supplication as discussed in this lesson? Can you come up with other possible differences?
8. Does Rom. 10:1 show there is a difference between desire and prayer? If so, how?
9. In expressing one's desires to God, must one always audibly speak to God? What passages of Scripture support your answer?
10. What truth about worship shows that the practice of praying to "saints" is wrong?

11. Is prayer a separate and distinct act of worship? Can you show this from Scripture?
12. What is an intercessory prayer? Illustrate the meaning of intercessory prayer from John 17.
13. Write before each passage below the kind of prayer referred to, using the following letters: I = intercession, S = supplication, T = thanksgiving, C = confession, and A = adoration (praise).

__1 Chron. 4:9-10
__ Ps. 51:1-4
__ Gen. 44:33
__ Lk. 23:34
__ Jn. 12:27
__ Jn. 11:41
__ Matt. 6:9,13
__ Job 42:1-6
__ Matt. 6:11
__ Rom. 1:9
__ Ps. 115:1
__ Mk. 8:6
__ 2 Cor. 12:8
__ I Sam. 15:24
__ Matt. 11:25
__ Gen, 18:16-33

___ Dan. 6:10
___ Ps. 84
___Gen, 24:27
___ Exod. 18:10-11

14. Do the following passages of Scripture teach that prayer may be addressed to Jesus? Matt. 8:2; 9:18; 28:9, 17; Lk. 24:52; Jn. 9:38; 20:28.
15. What is the main reason Christians fail to give thanks to God?
16. What is the central lesson taught in the passage where Jesus asked, "Where are the nine?" (Lk. 17:11-19)?
17. How much attention do you feel brethren give to praising God in prayer? Enough, or not enough?
18. Do we really pray for one another (intercession) as we ought?

2

Does Prayer Really Work?

It was Tennyson who said, "More things are wrought by prayer than this world dreams of." If only one knew all the good accomplished and the evil averted through prayer, but there is no concrete way to measure it. Only eternity will tell some of the things we wish we knew now. James says, "The supplication of a righteous man availeth much in its working" (Jas. 5:16b). Even though we do not always know exactly when, or even how, prayer is working for us, we have the assurance of Scripture that it does. Let's analyze this statement from James and then give some consideration to the difficulties involved in the subject.

PRAYER WORKS FOR THE CHRISTIAN

We sometimes ask, "Is there power in prayer?" By this question we mean, "Does prayer really work?" James says it does. Jesus assured His apostles that prayer works when He said to them, "And whatsoever ye shall ask in my name, that will I do" (Jn. 14:13, 14). Prayer was not meant only for the apostles. It is meant for all Christians for all time. James was not talking about apostles when he said prayer "availeth much in its working." He said prayer avails much for "a righteous man." When Paul admonished the Philippians to pray, he did not speak to apostles but to Christians. To the Christians in Philippi he said, "In nothing be anxious; but in everything by prayer and supplication with thanksgiving let your requests be made known to God" (Phil. 4:6). These passages, as well as other passages like them, would be meaningless if after the last apostle had died God stopped answering prayers.

In James 5:16b the terms "avails much" and "effectual fervent" appear in the King James Version. But Albert Barnes states:

> The word *effectual* is not the most happy translation here, since it seems to do little more than to state a truism that a prayer which is *effectual is availing*—that is, that it is effectual. The Greek word ... would be better rendered by the word energetic, which is indeed derived from it. The word properly refers to that which has power; which in its own nature is fitted to produce an effect.

Barnes, in other words, believes the idea in the word is that the prayer that is suited to produce an effect is the prayer that is sincere, earnest, hearty and persevering, not the prayer that is listless, indifferent, cold, or lifeless, as if there were no vitality or power in it.

Lenski agrees and translates it as follows: "A righteous one's petition avails when putting forth its energy." J. W. Roberts also adopts this view. He says:

> ... James means that a prayer which is 'working, operative or doing' is the prayer which is very strong or prevailing with God ... The petition of a righteous man avails when it is doing its work, which is petitioning, pleading, begging. The action of prayer must be earnestly and persistently engaged in. God does not want to interpret our own desires and thoughts; he wants us to express them. Prayer is often an unused asset....

But others have expressed a different view on the meaning of this word. This difference is evident in the following translations: "in its working" (ASV), "in its effects" (RSV), "in its operation" (James Adamson, NIC), "in its working" (John Edward Ruther, Meyer's Com. on N.T.), and, of course, many others with the same or similar meaning. This view has been recently defended at length by James Adamson in *The New International Greek Testament Commentary* (see his Excursus I, pp. 205-210). His concluding statement is:

> ... Apart from everything else, ... (Greek word here omitted, ww) in James 5:16 is better taken to mean "in operation" than taken as a passive: this prayer is mighty in what it is able to do, not in what it is enabled to do. This latter is not without any indication of the source from which the power is alleged to be derived. We know that all strength does come from God; but there is a natural feeling that a righteous man's prayer, like Elijah's prayer (it was a curse), carries a mighty punch. So we translate: 'the prayer of a righteous man is very powerful in its operation.'

SOME DIFFICULTIES INVOLVED

Whether James is talking about prevailing prayer or the power of prayer, all true Christians believe in the efficacy of prayer. Such passages as Matthew 7:7-11, Matthew 21:22 with Mark 11:24, Philippians 4:6 and others plainly teach that there is power in prayer. But even those who believe in the efficacy of prayer are not so presumptuous as to assume that there are no problems involved on the subject of prayer working for the Christian. There are areas of the subject which no thinking person would claim to be able to treat to the full satisfaction of all. How could they when (along with the best of minds through the centuries) human understanding is so limited on the subject of prayer. This limited understanding should not deter us in our study, but it should humble us.

Limited Information. The study of prayer should be approached in the same way that any subject that has not been fully revealed to us by God is studied. Our study can go only so far as the information goes. The Bible does not propose to reveal everything there is to know about prayer any more than it claims to make known all there is to know about God, creation or miracles. It affirms many things which it does not seek to prove logically.

Take as an example the fact that the Bible affirms that God exists (Gen. 1:1), but it does not then set out to establish through a logical process proof of this affirmation. This does not mean that the Bible is illogical in what it affirms about God on this matter. The Bible is quite logical in what it does affirm with regard to God's existence, but the point is, it does not upon having made this affirmation then go to great lengths to prove it. It assumes the proposition it has made without arguing the point for the skeptical mind.

The same may be said for miracles. The Bible claims that miracles have been one of the ways in which God has worked at times in history, but it does not give us a precisely worded definition of a miracle, nor does it explain exactly how miracles are possible in a world that is kept in place and continues to operate according to what commonly is called the "laws of nature." In the same way, the Bible teaches that there is power in prayer for the righteous person who prays to God in faith. Jesus, for example, teaches that we ought to pray even for those things which God already knows we need (Matt. 6:8, 32). He also shows us how we ought to pray (Matt. 6:9-13). But He nowhere attempts to show us how it is possible for God to answer our prayers in a world where miracles are not used, nor does He tackle such excruciating problems as how it is possible to reconcile the apparent conflict between the sovereignty of God and the necessity of prayer.

We are not however left completely unarmed as we face these problems on the subject of prayer, any more than we are on the subjects of God's existence and miracles. Without trying to be God or attempting to speak authoritatively where the Bible is silent, we do believe that some things can be said that will prove to be of some help to us as we face some of these problem areas.

Prayer and the Sovereignty of God. In the first place, we must remember that truth is not to be weighed in a pair of scales balancing the duty of prayer against the difficulty of the sovereignty of God, as though one can be canceled by the other. The only way one can dismiss prayer as necessary is to successfully remove the evidence (in this case, the clear affirmations of Scripture) on which the necessity of prayer rests. Simply introducing a difficulty will not remove the duty nor prove its invalidity for today. Such difficulties usually arise because the subject so far transcends the limits of our finite comprehension, not because there is in fact a conflict within the subject itself.

We do best to avoid extremes in the handling of difficulties of this sort. For some people God simply cannot act in the world except as He has already decreed before the foundation of the world. This theory of God's actions in the world is absolutely necessary, according to them, or else God's sovereignty is jeopardized. If we are to accept this view of God's relation to His creation, however, it would seem to make prayer a meaningless exercise. What possible meaning could prayer have if God has already decided, solely on the basis of His divine will, every event in history and every act of man which shall transpire in time and eternity?

It is no discredit to the sovereignty of God to say that God does some things in response to prayer which He had not planned before the foundation of the world. The fact that God is to some degree conditioned by man's acts does not make Him any less God. Nathan E. Wood makes this point well in the following words:

> God is conditioned by the fact that there are human souls. It is not derogatory to His infinite sovereignty to say that He is conditioned in His relation with men, by the will of man. It is a condition which He chose to put upon Himself when He created men free moral beings. He certainly is a right judge as to whether or

> not such condition is derogatory to His sovereignty ... God acts omnipotently but always within limits which preserve man's moral freedom and responsibility.

If God is limited by our unbelief and disobedience, as Scripture itself affirms (Ps. 78:41), we should not think it such an incredible thing that God may be moved by our sincere requests and our acts of obedience to grant us blessings according to our needs.

> The weary ones had rest, the sad had joy
>   That day, and wondered "how?"
> A ploughman singing at his work, had prayed
>   "Lord, help them now."
>
> Away in foreign lands they wondered "how"
>   Their simple words had power;
> At home, the Christians, two or three, had met
>   To pray an hour.
>
> Yes, we are always wondering, wondering "how,"
>   Because we do not see
> Someone, unknown perhaps, and far away,
>   On bended knee.

QUESTIONS FOR JOY AND PROFIT

1. What promise did Jesus make to His apostles regarding prayer?
2. Is this same promise made to all Christians?

3. How embracing is the word "everything" in Philippians 4:6?
4. What is the meaning of the word "efficacy"? Must Christians believe in the efficacy of prayer?
5. What does James mean by "supplication" in James 5:16?
6. Who is the "righteous man" referred to in this passage?
7. What point does Albert Barnes make about the words "effectual" and "avails" in the King James rendering of this passage? Is it a valid point?
8. What is the difference in meaning in this passage as it is translated by Lenski and Adamson?
9. Which view does the following translations represent? Put an "L" in the blank if it agrees with Lenski and an "A" if it agrees with Adamson.

    ___"The prayer of a righteous man has great power in its effects"

    ___"The petition of a righteous man is strong, being made effective"

    ___"The supplication of a righteous man availeth much in its working"

___"An upright man can do a great deal by prayer when he tries"

___"Very powerfully productive is the prayer of a righteous man"

___"For the unceasing prayer of a just man is of great avail"

___"The inwrought prayer of a righteous man avails much"

___"The prayers of the righteous have a powerful effect"

___"The effective prayer of a righteous man can accomplish much"

___"The prayer of a righteous man is powerful and effective"

10. Whichever of these two views is correct on the meaning of this word, does the Bible teach that prayer must be prevailing (Lk. 11:5-8; 18:1-8), and that prayer has great effects also (Jas. 5:17-18)?

11. What are some passages that teach that there is great power in prayer?

12. In what way is it true that we have limited information on the subject of prayer?

13. Are there other subjects like prayer about which we have limited information?

14. Does the Bible attempt to "prove" the existence of God?
15. Does the Bible explain "how" prayer can be answered without miracles and in a world governed by natural laws?
16. Does the Bible attempt to reconcile the apparent conflict between the necessity of prayer and the sovereignty of God?
17. What is the sovereignty of God?
18. What is meant by the statement that God is conditioned by man's acts? Do you agree with this statement?
19. What is the central point made in the poem at the end of this lesson?

3

What in the World is God Doing?

The idea of an arbitrary sovereignty of God in relation to man's actions has been seen to be altogether inconsistent with the character of God and the free agency of man. Such a view of the Divine will would also be inconsistent with the facts of God's providence. Every Christian believes that God is doing something in the world, and that His action is always based upon His Divine will for His creation. The question is, what is God doing in the world?

The expression "will of God" appears often in Scripture. It does not always have the same meaning in each appearance. At least two meanings may be clearly identified. Sometimes it refers to what God has said in, or attempts to accomplish through, Scripture. At other times it speaks of God's purposeful actions in the world outside the pages of His revealed will.

THE REVEALED WILL OF GOD

Hebrews 10:7 makes a clear reference to the will of God as it is revealed in Scripture. At the place where this verse appears the writer of Hebrews shows how God disapproved of mere animal sacrifices as valueless in themselves. He tells us that God prepared Christ's body so that He might perform the will of God. God had revealed His will and had it recorded in "the volume of the book," that is, in Scripture. The Scripture is viewed in this passage as making known the will of God; it is the will of God expressed to man. Verse 10 says that we are also sanctified "by this will," speaking of the same will just referred to. The Bible speaks of knowing God's will (Acts 22:14; Rom. 2:18) and doing the will of God (Matt. 7:21; Jn. 4:34; 7:17; 9:31; Eph. 6:6; Heb. 10:7, 9, 36; 1 Jn. 2:17).

Moses, speaking to Israel, said, "The secret things belong unto God: but those things which are revealed belong unto us and to our children forever, that we may do all the words of this law" (Deut. 29:29). One does not know God's providential will in advance. He simply acknowledges and accepts the vicissitudes of life believing that finally God's will for him will be accomplished. God has revealed the things He wants us to know and do. We simply busy ourselves in doing the things He has revealed and trust that God will providentially use us as He judges best.

> Fear him, ye saints, and you will then
> Have nothing else to fear;
> Make you his service your delight,
> He'll make your wants his care.

THE PROVIDENTIAL WILL OF GOD

To speak of God's providential will is to talk about what God is doing in the world beyond the pages of Scripture. Through Jesus Christ, Paul tells us, God created the world, and "in him all things consist" (Col. 1:15-17). The footnote on the word "consist" in the American Standard Version says, "That is, hold together." Christ both sustains the universe and is the unifying principle of its life. The words of R. E. O. White are aptly put: "In Him they hold together;

by Him all things consist, find their inner coherence, and their final meaning. Without Christ the universe is no longer meaningful, or viable: He is its meaning, its coherence, and its life." This point will be more fully developed in our next two lessons.

Simply defined, the word providence means the superintending care which God exercises over creation. The idea expressed in this definition is not hard to conceive, and it is generally believed by all professed Christians. The extent of God's providential activity however, and how God works providentially in a world where miracles have ceased, has been a subject of much discussion for centuries. What in the world is God doing? We may not find answers which completely satisfy us, but one thing is certain: if we are to believe what the Bible teaches about prayer, we must believe in the providence of God.

> One prayer I have — all prayers in one —
>   When I am wholly thine:
> Thy will, my God, thy will be done,
>   And let that will be mine;
> All-wise, almighty, and all-good,
>   In thee I firmly trust,
> Thy ways, unknown or understood,
>   Are merciful and just.

The Bible teaches that God gives wisdom to those who ask in faith (Jas. 1:5-8); He gives greater grace to, and exalts, those who are humble (Jas. 4:6, 10); He raises up the sick in response to prayer offered in faith (Jas. 5:13-18); He has ultimate control over life and death (Jas. 4:15); He gives rain to the just and unjust (Matt. 5:45); He gives from heaven "rains and fruitful seasons, filling ... hearts with food and gladness" (Acts 14:17); He gives good things to His children when they ask, seek and knock (Matt. 7:7); He gives things necessary to our well-being when we pray, "Give us this day our daily bread" (Matt. 6:11).

A good summary statement on the providence of God is given by Jesus Himself in Matthew 6:19-34, a part of which reads: "But if God doth so clothe the grass of the field, which today is and tomorrow is cast into the oven, shall he not much more clothe you, O ye of little faith? Be not therefore anxious, saying, What shall we eat? or, What shall we drink? or, Wherewithal shall we be clothed? For after all these things do the Gentiles seek: for your heavenly Father knoweth that ye have need of all these things, But seek ye first his kingdom, and his righteousness, and all these things shall be added unto you" (vv. 30-33).

"IF THE LORD WILLS"

Life is viewed in the Scriptures as being under God's control. It is uncertain because we cannot know the future. We do not know whether we will live tomorrow, or die. God has the ultimate control over life and death. It's a matter of what God wills for us. James says, "You ought to say, 'If the Lord wills, we shall live and also do this or that'" (Jas. 4:15). Man must not only take into account what God's revealed will is for him, but he must also acknowledge God's providential control over his life.

Great men and women of faith have always been committed to both the revealed and providential will of God. Paul, a great man of faith, gave his life in teaching others God's revealed will. He was wholly committed to the word of truth which he preached. He completely depended upon the revealed truth as the norm by which his life was regulated. Yet he was equally committed to God's providential will for him personally. He planned his life in advance and hoped to be able to live in accordance with the plans he had made. He realized however that only God could make this possible. Every plan he made and every activity he hoped to engage in was always thought of in terms of what the Lord would choose for him. If he planned to return to Ephesus, it was "if God wills" (Acts 18:21); if he could not be persuaded by the brethren in Caesarea not to go to Jerusalem, it was because he had been "prospered by the will of God" to do so (Rom. 1:10); if he should be able to come to Corinth in a short while, it would be because "the Lord wills" (1 Cor. 4:19); if he is allowed to tarry a while with the Corinthians, it will be determined by the Lord Himself: "if the Lord permit" (1 Cor. 16:7).

> The best will is our Father's will,
> And we may rest there calm and still;
> O make it hour by hour thine own,
> And wish for naught but that alone
>   which pleases God.

In these ways Paul did exactly what James says every Christian should do. He made his plans knowing full well that he might not live to complete them, or that God might providentially lead him into other places to accomplish a work that was more urgent at the moment. It was not that Paul simply said, "If the Lord wills." To merely say these words is not the point James is getting at, and this was not all that Paul was doing. Paul made every plan with the certainty that it depended upon the providential hand of God for its accomplishment. A sense of dependence upon God and an acceptance of His will for our lives is essential if we are to live submissively to God. This was the key to Paul's success and it is the secret for successful Christian living for any Christian who would live faithfully before God.

What in the world is God doing? We may by way of summary classify God's activity in the world into three categories.

First, through Jesus Christ He is upholding the universe by His power, and He is giving meaning and life to His creation.

Second, through His revealed will He is saving people from their sins. James tells us that every good and perfect gift comes from God (Jas. 1:17). The specific example of a good and perfect gift from God is that God by His own will brought us forth by the word of truth (Jas. 1:18).

The words "brought forth" refer to a birth, and, of course, here it speaks of the new birth. Salvation from sin is often referred to under the figure of a birth in the New Testament (Jn. 3:1-8; 1 Cor. 4:15; 1 Pet. 1:22-23). One is born "of God," and it is "of his own will" that he is brought forth.

But the new birth is not brought about without the instrumentality of the word of God because James says God brought us forth "by the word of truth." This process of the new birth also involves a response in faith and obedience on man's part when the revealed will of God is made known to him (Rom. 10:17; Mk. 16:15-16; Acts 2:37-38). Christians are then built up through the teaching of the revealed will of God (Acts 20:32; 1 Thess. 2:13; 1 Pet. 2:1-2; 2 Pet. 3:18).

Finally, God is working providentially in the world. How this is possible in a world where miracles have ceased and the laws of nature seem to have already determined the operations of the universe will be the subject of our next two chapters.

> The shuttles of His purpose move
> To carry out His own design;
> Seek not too soon to disapprove
> His work, nor yet assign
> Dark motives, when, with silent tread
> You view some somber fold;
> For lo, within each darker thread
> There twines a thread of gold.
> Spin cheerfully,
> Not tearfully,
> He knows the way you plod;
> Spin carefully,
> Spin prayerfully,
> But leave the thread with God.

QUESTIONS FOR JOY AND PROFIT

1. What is the revealed will of God?
2. Does Hebrews 10:7, 10 speak of this aspect of God's will? If so, how?
3. What is the point made about knowing and doing the will of God?
4. What is a simple definition of providence?
5. Is providence a work of God carried out through Scripture?
6. What are some passages of Scripture that speak of the providential will of God?
7. What is the significance of Deuteronomy 29:29 to this subject?
8. Do most Christians believe in the providence of God?
9. What kind of questions are the hardest to answer on the subject of God's providence?
10. What has Christ done and what does he continue to do in relation to the universe, according to Colossians 1:17?
11. What are the implications of this in light of what we call the laws of nature?
12. From the list of passages given below jot down what God promises to do and any conditions involved, if such conditions are given.

PASSAGE	PROMISE	CONDITION(S)
Matt. 7:7		
Jas. 5:13-18		
Matt. 6:11		
Jas. 4:6, 10		
Jas. 4:13-16		
Matt. 6:30-33		
Jas. 1:5-8		
Acts 14:17		

13. What is the meaning of James 4:15, "If the Lord wills, we shall live and also do this or that." To what extent does God have control over life, death and the things we do?
14. How was Paul committed to the revealed will of God?
15. Was Paul committed to God's providential will? What does this mean? Illustrate your answer.
16. How was Paul "prospered by the will of God" to go to Rome? Through the pages of Scripture, or in some other way?

17. What is the meaning of the often repeated statement, "If the Lord wills," for Paul? Is this something Paul simply said, or is more involved in this?
18. What was the key to Paul's success? To ours?
19. In our summary statement, what three things were noted that God is doing in the world?
20. What is the meaning of James 1:17? In what way does James illustrate the claim made in this passage?
21. What is the instrument used by God to bring about the new birth?
22. Is obedience on man's part essential to be born of God? If salvation is "of His own will", how can it also be of the will of man? How can it be a gift of God and yet man be required to respond in faith and obedience?

4

How in the World Is God Doing It? (I)

J. W. McGarvey, an able, well known and much loved gospel preacher of the past, said that the skepticism regarding prayer in his day grew out of peoples' own nearsightedness.

> We look around and think of the laws of nature, and remember that God does not work miracles in this day, and we don't see how God can alter things to suit our wishes and petitions. We are told he is an unchanging God; how can he then answer prayer? Thus we set limits to God's ability to act without doing miracles. God can bring about certain things by miracles, and it seems reasonable to suppose that he can do some things without a miracle.

Times have not changed significantly since the day that McGarvey wrote these words. If any change has occurred it would be more in the direction of a greater hardening against belief in God's ability to do anything in the world today. Even those who avow a strong belief in God have a hard time with this question.

INFLUENCED BY OUR AGE

Christians are too often influenced by the character of the times in which they live. It is so easy for us to find ourselves being molded into the thinking of the world around us. There are those in every age who set the pattern and mold the character of the times in which they live, and Christians are ever in danger of being formed into the mold or pattern which they set. Paul refers to such pattern makers in 1 Corinthians 2:6, 8 when he speaks of "the rulers of this world."

By the word "rulers" Paul makes specific reference to those who crucified Christ, but these are only representative of the larger class Paul has in mind in using this term. The "rulers" are those in any age who determine the character of this world. They include the great thinkers, the philosophers, sociologists, politicians, and the leaders in the fields of science and art. How these leaders think determines the "wisdom" of the times in which we live, and almost invariably it is a wisdom which is opposed to the "wisdom of God" that was being preached by Paul in Corinth. No wonder Paul admonishes Christians not to "be fashioned according to this world: but be ye transformed by the renewing of your mind, that ye may prove what is the good and acceptable and perfect will of God" (Rom. 12:2).

Most all of the great schools of thought and the various fields of science have an important role to play in the world. Religion is not at war with true science. But when science, philosophy or politics makes no room for religion it has in its "wisdom" rejected the "wisdom of God," and this is what has happened in most cases. That would not be so bad in itself, but, sadly, far too many people conform to the pattern set by these leaders. Most people become children of their age—their materialistic age—and with the leaders of this world share the skepticism that is characteristic of their time.

IS ANSWERED PRAYER REASONABLE IN LIGHT OF OUR ADVANCED KNOWLEDGE ABOUT THE WORLD?

But how can God do anything for us in answer to prayer in a world that is kept in motion by laws that are constant and invariable, laws which we refer to as "the laws of nature"? Is it reasonable to believe in the power of prayer today when in our advanced knowledge about the world we know that the operations of this world are "fixed" according to a determined pattern of natural laws? Even the very best of Christians have had this question to arise in their minds at one time or another. Elton Trueblood gives a quite vivid description of this attitude in the following words:

> The greatest difficulty is felt in connection with petition and intercession. Men have long prayed for rain, but how can this be done with intellectual honesty when we realize something of the nature of meteorology? Men have long prayed for the restoration of the health of their loved ones, but how can this be done by honest persons who know something of the action of germs? When a person has pneumonia what is needed, it would seem, is not prayer, but antibiotics. Such

considerations do not, of course, prevent recourse to prayer, but they hinder it. Most parents, it is probable, pray for a child who is in danger of contracting infantile paralysis, but many wonder, in doing so, if they are acting rationally.

The difficulty is most clear when the time factor is involved. If a person receives a letter and, before opening it, prays that the letter may not contain bad news, the prayer has no justification. Whatever is in the letter is there already, and nothing under heaven will change it. In other words, such a prayer is self-contradictory. It asks that what is, be something other than what it is. But the same difficulty remains in less obvious situations. Prayer about the contents of the letter is pointless at any time after it is written.

Much of our uneasiness in regard to other areas, such as the physical and biological, arises from the conviction that the situation is already as fully determined by natural laws as the contents of the letter are already fixed by the writer. Whether there will be rain is already in the cards. But if this is true for one day, why not for a million? In the same way, the ravages of a disease seem to be already determined by the introduction of germs. In short, it is always too late. Perhaps, then, prayer is merely an irrational survival of a superstitious and anthropomorphic age. In that case, it will eventually cease with the growth of intelligence or continue as a sentimental gesture, but nothing more.

Whether prayer seems rational to the modern mind will in a large measure be determined by one's view of natural law and God's relation to His creation. Various attempts have been made to explain God's relation to the world, some of them totally unacceptable to the Christian point of view because they would rule out any place for prayer or the providence of God in the world. Yet, surprisingly enough, many Christians have been influenced in one way or another by these views. They have (perhaps unknowingly) in wrestling with this difficulty fallen into the mold which has been set by the rulers of this world.

The pantheist holds that matter is God, and all life and thought are but modes of His operation. This view of God and the world denies intelligence, sensibility or will, as well as consciousness or personality, to God. The pantheist therefore makes no allowance for a work of creation or providence. Prayer in this system of thought would, of course, make no sense.

The deist, who believes in the personality of God and His creative work, but denies God's providence, says the world is much like a clock: God wound it up at the time of creation, but

He then left it to run on its own from that time forward. This view of God and the world also makes prayer meaningless.

Is God so withdrawn from the physical creation, as the deist contends, that He is not involved in any way with what is going on in this universe? Even brethren sometimes wonder as if this might be the case. We hear people speak of praying for spiritual things but not for physical things. Why would people who believe the Bible talk like that? Do such ideas about prayer come from the Bible? If so, what does the Bible teach about God, the universe, miracles, natural law, or prayer that would lead to such a conclusion? It is not from the Bible that one would draw such conclusions. It sounds like some professed Christians have fallen prey to the naturalistic way of thinking about God, the physical order and prayer.

Does the Bible separate the physical realm from the spiritual realm to such an extent that God's involvement in the one makes it impossible for Him to be involved in the other? Are we to view the working of this physical universe as "fixed" or so locked up, so to speak, that God's hands are tied so that He cannot involve Himself in the world without working a miracle? Are the so-called laws of nature outside of God's control?

There are laws that govern the spiritual realm just as there are laws that govern the physical realm. One could reasonably affirm that just as there are laws that govern both realms, so God's relation to both realms is such that if He cannot answer prayer in one realm, He cannot answer prayer with regard to the other. God either has established the laws of both realms and maintains control over them both, and therefore is quite capable of answering prayer in relation to both, or He does not govern in either realm and, as a consequence, cannot answer prayer in relation to either.

GOD AND HIS CREATION

When God created the physical universe He created it *ex nihilo,* that is, out of nothing. "By faith we understand that the worlds have been framed by the word of God, so that what is seen hath not been made out of things which appear" (Heb. 11:3). It is simply not conceivable that once the world of space and time had been created God then completely severed Himself from it. It was dependent upon Him in its origin, according to the passage we have just quoted, and it is dependent upon Him in its continuance, as we shall see. This means that all things originated with God, and if they continue it is due to His continued presence and activity.

It may be affirmed then that the *ex nihilo* creation logically necessitates a coexistence of the material and spiritual. Yet, it is not merely coexistence, but a dependent relationship of the physical upon the spiritual. The kind of severance some seem to find between the physical and the spiritual is not founded on anything taught in Scripture. With this kind of relationship between God and His creation one should not have great difficulty in seeing how God can as easily answer prayer which pertains to the physical realm as He can in the spiritual realm.

Christ existed before the creation of all things, but it is also true that "by him all things consist" (Col. 1:17). In other words, Christ, as the agent of God in creation, brought all things into existence in the beginning, but, according to this verse, all things which He created also continue to hold together through Him. E. H. Andrews draws the following valid conclusion from this verse:

Our Scripture therefore states that Christ prexisted the material, and, indeed, the angelic creation and 'in Him' all created things hold together. Everything derives its being and integrity from the presence and activity of the Second Person of the Trinity. Earlier I said that all science can be reduced to laws, and that law describes interaction. This interaction conveys just the same idea as the word 'consists', so that we may claim direct scriptural authority for the view that the entire physical world derives its being and behaviour from the presenttense activity of the triune God.

Surely God can answer prayer for people who live in space and time, even when their prayers involve "things" tied in with space and time, if God Himself is the source of this world's origin as well as its continuance on a day to day basis.

God of the earth, the sky, the sea,
Of all above and all below,
Creation lives and moves in thee,
Thy present life through all doth flow.

Thy love is in the sunshine's glow,
Thy life is in the quickening air;
When lightnings flash and storm-winds blow,
There is thy power, thy law is there.

> We feel thy calm at evening's hour,
> Thy grandeur in the march of night;
> And when the morning breaks in power,
> We hear thy word, "Let there be light!"
>
> But higher far, and far more clear,
> Thee in man's spirit we behold;
> Thine image and thyself are there,
> The indwelling God, proclaimed of old.

QUESTIONS FOR JOY AND PROFIT

1. How do people set limits to God's ability to act without doing miracles?
2. Who are the rulers of 1 Corinthians 2:6, 8? According to the context (1:18-2:16), what kind of wisdom do they espouse? In contrast to what?
3. What does it mean for one to become a child of the age in which he lives? What characterizes most ages in this world?
4. Is all doubt wrong? Was Thomas an honest doubter (Jn. 20:24-29)? Is there a difference between honest inquiry and skepticism?
5. We will study the meaning of natural law in our next chapter, but before reading it try to put in your own words what these terms mean to you.

6. What is the central point in the quotation from Elton Trueblood?
7. When does a prayer become self-contradictory?
8. Have you ever prayed for rain or for someone who is sick but wondered how it could do any good in view of your understanding of natural law?
9. How much do you think this problem has affected how strong peoples' faith is in prayer today?
10. What is pantheism? What does it deny about God? Would prayer have any significance in this system of thought? Why?
11. What is deism? Consult a good English dictionary for your definition.
12. What does the deist believe about God's relation to the universe? How does prayer fit into this system? Why?
13. Is it reasonable to believe that God can answer prayer for physical things?
14. What do we mean when we speak of the spiritual realm and the physical realm? Are these related in any way to each other? How?

15. Should it be just as easy for God to do something for us in one realm as in the other? Why?
16. What is creatio ex nihilo? What verse, if any, teaches this doctrine?
17. What significance does this doctrine of creation have on this subject?
18. What is meant by a coexistence of the material and spiritual?
19. What does Colossians 1:17 teach about the continuance of this universe?
20. What bearing does this have on the subject of prayer?

5

How in the World Is God Doing It? (II)

We are looking at God's present relation to the universe. We have seen that through Christ God's creation is held together (Col. 1:17). The entire physical world derives its being and behavior from the present-tense activity of God. Because God Himself is spirit and the whole physical creation derives its being and continuance from Him, it is reasonable to assume that prayer has validity in the physical realm as well as in the spiritual. This was the point of our discussion in the previous lesson.

To go a step further we may note that according to the Bible the world not only derives its being and continuance from God's presence in creation, but from the immediate word of

His power. Hebrews 1:3 says that Christ is (note the present tense of the word) "upholding all things by the word of his power." This means that things in this world are able to continue only on the basis of the very commands of God, His instantaneous word of power.

In view of this biblical claim, it might be well for us to take a closer look at our definition of natural law. It is likely true that one's definition of natural law and miracle often proves to be the greatest obstacle in the path to belief in God's ability to do anything in answer to prayer in today's world. If we view natural law as an invisible, impersonal force, a force that is self-originating and self-sustaining, then to our minds it would logically follow that it would be very difficult, if not impossible, to see how God could do anything in answer to prayer without working a miracle. Beginning with such a view of natural law, we would likely also define miracles in such a way that any involvement on God's part in this physical world would to us be miraculous.

But what if we begin by defining natural law as but another expression of God's will, the very thing Hebrews 1:3 seems to say, "upholding all things by the word of his power"? Would this help us understand how it is possible for God to work providentially in the world?

A SEARCH FOR CONSISTENCY AND MEANING

The words "natural law" have been around for centuries, and they have been defined in many different ways. It is important that however we define these words our definition be consistent with what the Bible teaches about God's relation to the world and prayer. The definition we settle on here will not necessarily solve all the problems on the subject of prayer and the providence of God. We are simply looking for consistency. Whether we arrive at the most consistent view is a matter that must be determined by each person who grapples with this problem. It may not seem to be the most consistent view to everybody, but, at least, it seems to us that it is better to have tried and failed in somebody else's judgment than not to have tried at all. Augustine is reported to have said, "I had rather be found limping in the way than not to be in the way."

There are other courses that one could take that would seem to us to be worse than to try to come up with the most consistent approach to this subject and yet fall short of completely arriving at a perfectly consistent view. For one thing, it seems far better to strive for consistency with what the Bible teaches on prayer and providence, on the one hand, and how we are to define natural law, on the other, than to insist on a view of natural law that forces one to either believe in miracles today, or in denying miracles in our time, to give up belief in prayer and providence. Another equally unacceptable approach would be to define natural law in such a way that it plainly contradicts what we know the Bible teaches about God's relation to the world.

But, again: What if we define natural law simply as one of the ways in which God expresses His will? What would we then find? First, we would find that this definition would be in perfect harmony with what the Bible says about God's relation to the world: Christ upholds all things by the WORD of His power (Heb. 1:3). It would mean that God is sustaining this universe in all of its manifestations through what we call natural laws. Natural law in this definition is equated with the word of divine power. It is one of God's ways of doing things, not an impersonal force which is self-originating and self-sustaining.

Second, so far as we can judge, this definition of natural law is in no way inconsistent with the regularity and uniformity that we observe in the universe. We would expect that the very nature of the universe would demand that a certain amount of order be maintained. The universe could not exist, nor could it long continue in operation, without doing so as a unit. Each "law" in force in this world, so far as man is able to observe, is dependent upon every other "law". This is so whether we regard nature's "laws" as inherent in matter or the constant operation of God's will. The steady action of these forces would seem to be a necessary condition to the harmony of the universe.

But this does not mean that the physical laws of this universe are inexorable. It should be observed that throughout the paragraph above we have used such words as "so far as we can judge," "we would expect," "so far as man is able to observe," and "would seem to be." The truth of the matter is that our understanding of natural law is still quite elementary and incomplete. How is man with his limited knowledge of the universe to make absolute judgments about God's doings in His own creation? God may at times seem to defy the laws of the universe, but how can we be certain that He is not working within the created order? What seems to be inexorable laws to us may not be so in fact because conclusions about the universe are based upon immanent knowledge, or what is commonly referred to as a world-picture.

From the human standpoint it is generally conceded by the scientific world today that there are no such things as physical laws being absolute and unalterable; the reason for this being, that physical laws are today viewed as being nothing but the generalized product of our observations. The result has been that the word "miracle" is no longer defined by apologists of the Christian faith as an event contrary to the laws of nature.

If natural law then is nothing more than an observed order of sequence, the generalizations about the way things happen, with our limited knowledge about how things do happen, we cannot make absolute statements about the laws of nature.

We should rather speak in terms of things happening in this universe in a certain way most of the time; or, in our generalizations about the way things happen we should say this is the way things almost always happen. Since nature is the way God decides force shall act on matter by His will most of the time, and laws are merely our descriptions of what does happen, then God's providential acts are but the ways in which God accomplishes His will in the world through these chosen channels. A miracle is wrought when God works above and beyond these ordinary ways of acting in the world; or possibly through bringing about an event consequent upon a localized change in the laws of nature.

> The winds blow hard? What then?
> He holds them in the hollow of His hand;
> The furious blasts will sink when His command
>   Bids them be calm again.
>
> The night is dark? What then?
> To Him the darkness is as bright as day.
> At His command the shades will flee away,
>   And all be light again.
>
> The wave is deep? What then?
> For Israel's host the waters upright stood.
> And He whose power controlled that raging flood
>   Still succors helpless men.

A SEARCH FOR ACCEPTANCE

In the brief compass of these two chapters we of course cannot possibly touch on all the facets of such an involved subject as the providence of God. Our search is not merely a search for consistency and meaning, but it is in the final analysis a search for acceptance. Knowing that we are to "walk by faith, not by sight" (2 Cor. 5:7), we yet find ourselves crying out with the father who asked Jesus to cure his possessed child, "I believe; help thou mine unbelief"(Mk. 9:24). Having done the best we can to find the most consistent meaning of the terms involved on the subject of prayer and the providence of God, the thing that remains is simply to bring ourselves to accept what the Bible says about the subject, knowing that finally God's will will be accomplished for us.

This world of ours is not governed by law; it is governed by God according to law. As Harry Emerson Fosdick said, "He providentially utilizes, manipulates and combines his own invariable ways of acting to serve his own eternal purposes." During his lifetime Fosdick was a leading proponent of the liberal viewpoint, but he expressed in his book on prayer a very conservative position; a view that is outrightly rejected by the liberalism of our own day. Richard J. Coleman summarizes Fosdick's treatment of the subject as follows:

> When we pray for God's help, then, we are not asking him to disrupt the ordered universe but asking for his divine power to manifest itself in the operation of natural law. God is the master of all laws, known and unknown to us. When he utilizes his knowledge of his own laws, who can say in advance what is possible? God is free to answer any prayer whatsoever; and if a petition is not granted it is not because the reign of natural law prevents God from acting. The more likely explanation is that there are certain areas where God must not substitute our wish for his plan.

Various attempts have been made to explain suffering, as well as physical catastrophes such as earthquakes, volcanos and the like, and certain moral disasters like mass murders. Some have found help in attempting to distinguish between what they consider to be different aspects of God's will. They speak of God's intentional will, His circumstantial will and His ultimate will. Others think it is best to talk about the perfect and permissible will of God.

All such efforts, perhaps, have a place in wrestling with difficulties of this sort, but none seem to completely satisfy us, and after all has been said that can be said, we come back to the simple truth that God's ways in the world are not completely known to us, and even when known, many times they are beyond our understanding. Leslie D. Weatherhead quotes Canon Streeter as saying, "Evil is evil and loss is loss, but God has the power, out of, and through the evil and the loss, to bring good and gain, just as the farmer can make the filth of the midden the source of renewed fertility to his land." Weatherhead then attempts to illustrate the point with the making of a Persian rug. We conclude our discussion here with his description and application.

> When they are making a Persian rug, they put it up vertically on a frame, and little boys, sitting at various levels, work on the wrong side of it. The artist stands on the right side of the rug, the side on which people will tread, and shouts his instructions to the boys on the other side. Sometimes a boy will make a mistake in the rug ... I said to the student, 'What happens when the boy makes a mistake?'
>
> 'Well,' he said, 'quite often the artist does not make the little boy take out the

wrong color. If he is a great enough artist, he weaves the mistake into the pattern.'

Is there not here a parable of life? You and I are working on the wrong side of the rug. We cannot watch the pattern developing. I know I put in the wrong color very often. I put in black when God meant red, and yellow when he meant white; and the other workers with whom I make my rug make mistakes too. Sometimes I am tempted to say, 'Is there anybody on the other side of the rug; am I just left to make a mess of my life alone? Is there Anybody there?' Then, through the insight which comes back with returning faith, I realize that instead of making me undo it all or letting my life's purpose be ruined, God puts more in. I wonder sometimes if he alters the pattern? It isn't what it might have been; but because he is such a great Artist I haven't quite spoiled everything. So, at the end, when he calls me down off my plank and takes me round to the other side, I shall see that just because he is such a great Artist, no mistakes of mine can utterly spoil the pattern; nothing can divert his purpose ultimately, or finally spoil his plan. If only I will work with him, 'simply trusting every day,' I think one day I shall find my mistakes and my calamities and my distress and my failures and all my pain, woven into the pattern, and I shall say, 'It is the Lord's doing, and it is marvelous in our eyes.' Some such faith I must have to believe in a God of love who puts us into a world where things can go so utterly wrong.

God moves in a mysterious way,
His wonders to perform;
He plants His footsteps in the sea,
And rides upon the storm.

Deep in unfathomable mines
Of never failing skill,
He treasures up His bright designs,
And works His gracious will.

Ye fearful saints, fresh courage take,
The clouds ye so much dread
Are big with mercy, and shall break
In blessings on your head.

Judge not the Lord by feeble sense,
But trust Him for His grace;
Behind a frowning providence,
He hides a smiling face.

His purposes will ripen fast,
Unfolding every hour;
The bud may have a bitter taste,
But sweet will be the flow'r.

Blind unbelief is sure to err,
And scan His work in vain;
God is His own interpreter,
And He will make it plain.

QUESTIONS FOR JOY AND PROFIT

1. What is the meaning of Hebrews 1:3 as it pertains to this study? What is the "word of his power"?

2. What is natural law? What is nature? What is law in relation to nature?
3. What is miracle? Is miracle contrary to natural law? Why?
4. What is providence? Is an act of providence miraculous? Why?
5. How are natural laws, miracle and providence related to each other?
6. What is God's relation to each of these?
7. What is likely the greatest obstacle to belief in God's involvement in the world?
8. What do we mean by searching for consistency on this subject? Give an example of an inconsistent position (besides ours, if you think it is!).
9. If natural law is defined as one way in which God expresses His will, how does this harmonize with what the Bible says about God's relation to the world?
10. Does this definition of natural law conflict with the regularity and uniformity observed in the universe? If not, why?
11. Are natural laws inexorable?
12. What is a world-picture? How does this apply to the subject of physical laws in the universe?

13. Can we make absolute statements about the laws of nature? Why?
14. What does it mean to "walk by faith, and not by sight"?
15. What is the difference between the view of the liberal theologian Harry Emerson Fosdick and modern liberals on the subject of prayer?
16. How have some attempted to explain the goodness of God in light of natural disasters, suffering and moral crimes?
17. What is the significance of the quote from Canon Streeter?
18. What is the central point in the illustration from the making of a Persian rug?
19. How does the song, "God Moves in a Mysterious Way," quoted at the end of the lesson address the subject of God's will, judging God and unbelief?
20. What does Joseph say about God's providence in his own life in Genesis 45:5? How did God do this without working a miracle?
21. Does Esther 4:14 suggest that Esther was where she was because God had put her there for a specific purpose? How did God do this?

22. What does Daniel 4:35 say about God? What does Daniel say about God in Daniel 2:20-22?
23. As time permits discuss the following passages of Scripture: Rom. 11:33-38 and Acts 17:28a.

6

The Practice of Prayer

In studying prayer one may be profited immensely by studying about prayer, and he also may be greatly rewarded by studying the prayers that have been preserved for us in the Bible. The great heroes of faith in both the Old and New Testaments were people who strongly believed in prayer. Not many of their prayers have been recorded in the Bible, but from the ones that we do have it is evident that they not only believed in prayer, but their practice of prayer is a firm witness to their belief in it. A sampling of prayers from Abraham (Gen. 18:9-33), Jacob (Gen. 32:22-32), Moses (Ex. 32:9-14, 31-32; 33:12-23), David (Ps. 51), Daniel (Dan. 9:1-19), Hannah (1 Sam. 1:1-18), Job

(Job 38:1-7; 40:1-5; 42:1-6), Jesus (Matt. 26:36-46; 27:45-46; Lk. 23:34, 46; Jn. 17), and Paul (Eph. 1:15-23; 3:14-21) is sufficient to convince any fair-minded person that prayer was at the center of the lives of Bible characters who had their lives centered upon God.

A TIME TO PRAY

Most things that we do successfully are done as a result of long and continued practice. Great musicians, successful inventors, and outstanding writers and speakers have been recognized in their field of specialty because they have devoted themselves wholly to the one primary thing they have set their heart on accomplishing. One does not learn to do a thing well unless he does it over and over and over until he has perfected himself in it. The key to success in any worthwhile venture is summed up in three words—PRACTICE, PRACTICE, PRACTICE.

The development of Christian virtues is no exception. If we are to learn how to pray well, we must be in the habit of praying. We may know all there is to know about prayer, and we may even memorize all the prayers of the Bible, yet if we are not in the habit of praying we will not become successful at praying. A knowledge about prayer and familiarity with the great prayers of the Bible is necessary if we would learn how to pray. But prayer must also be practiced.

We do those things that are of importance to us. We must notice how important prayer was to our Lord even in the midst of a busy life. From some seventeen references to His active prayer-life one would gather that He did not take the matter of prayer lightly; it was one of the key elements in His successful ministry. No matter how busy he was He could immediately turn aside for long seasons of prayer. In fact, prayer was so habitual with Him, in one sense, His whole life seems to have been a prayer offered up to God. The times that were regularly given to prayer are a true index to His inner self. They reflect a habitual attitude of His mind and heart. When one's heart is continually directed toward God there is always a time to pray.

"MEN OUGHT ALWAYS TO PRAY"

In Luke 18:1 we read that Jesus "spake a parable unto them to the end that they ought always to pray, and not to faint." The word "ought" expresses a moral and spiritual obligation, not just an option. Praying regularly and often is an absolute necessity. That men ought to persist in prayer and not be discouraged in spite of the Lord's delay in coming, and that they should persevere in prayer even when the answer is not immediately granted, is taught in this parable (Lk. 18:2-8).

This same important lesson is often emphasized by Paul, who has much to say about prayer. He teaches us that our practice of prayer should be constant. He calls on the Ephesians to pray "at all seasons" (Eph. 6:18). The Christian must realize that his life is one of constant warfare, as the context here describes (Eph. 6:10-17). Constant prayer in preparation for and engagement in the battle is therefore required. The point seems to be that every incident in life is to be dealt with in prayer.

The need for "continuing steadfastly in prayer" (Rom. 12:12; Col. 4:2) is also introduced by Paul. This admonition to diligence in prayer must not be overlooked. Paul implies in the passage in Romans that such constancy in prayer is relevant to the two preceding injunctions: "rejoicing in hope" and "patient in tribulation". Charles

Hodge describes the relationship between these three exhortations as follows:

> These exhortations refer to nearly related duties: Christians are to be joyful, patient and prayerful. However adverse their circumstances, hope, patience and prayer are not only duties, but the richest sources of consolation and support. "Rejoicing on account of hope," or in the 'joyful expectation of future good.' This hope of salvation is the most effectual means of producing patience under present afflictions; for if we feel 'that the sufferings of this present time are not worthy to be compared with the glory which shall be revealed in us,' it will not be difficult to bear them patiently. Intercourse with God, however, is necessary to the exercise of this and all other virtues, and therefore the apostle adds, continuing instant in prayer .....

Paul himself prayed "always" for the Colossians (Col. 1:3) and "night and day" for the Thessalonians (1 Thess. 3:10). "Night and day" must mean continued prayer, not prayer at these two set times. The word "always" also gives the idea of constancy in prayer. Paul often writes of his unceasing prayers (1 Cor. 1:4; Eph. 1:15. 16; Phil. 1:3-5; Col. 1:3, 9). In writing to the Thessalonians, he exhorted them to pray "without ceasing" (1 Thess. 5:17), and assured them that it was without ceasing that he prayed for them (1 Thess. 1:2, 3; 2:13; 2 Thess. 1:3, 11, 12; 2:13-15).

HERE AND THERE AND EVERYWHERE

When we look into the life of the Lord, his apostles and the early church it is clear that their practice of prayer was indeed unlimited. We would expect to find only occasional references to their prayers, but in view of the scarcity of material that we have given to us about each Bible character, the number of references is rather large. The references are sufficient to convince us that prayer was one of their main sources of strength. They also make it clear to us that prayer was viewed by them as the best avenue open to them for expressing their total dependence upon God. A quick look at some of these examples will show us how true it is that Jesus and the early Christians viewed every incident in life as an event to be dealt with in prayer. This is, in fact, the real meaning of praying always and praying without ceasing.

Jesus prayed before all the great events in His life: at the time of His baptism (Lk. 3:21), before the call of the twelve (Lk. 6:12ff.), before Peter's confession (Lk. 9:18ff.), at the transfiguration (Lk. 9:29ff.). Often in the course of His ministry He prayed: before the great conflict with the religious leaders of His day (Lk. 5:16), before giving the model prayer for His disciples (Lk. 11:1), when the Greeks came and asked to see Jesus (Jn. 12:27ff.), at the time of the raising of Lazarus (Jn. 11:41), in connection with other miracles (Mk. 1:35; 6:41; 7:34), and often-times for other people (Jn. 17:6-19; 17:20-26; Lk. 22:32; 23:34).

The apostles and early church were also in the habit of constant prayer. The twelve were in prayer as they waited for the promise of the Holy Spirit (Lk. 24:46-49; Acts 1:4, 14, 26; 2:1). Peter was in prayer when he received a vision from God that the Gentiles are no longer to be considered unclean by him (Acts 10:9ff.). He prayed as life was restored to Dorcas (Acts 9:40-41). When Peter and John were released by the Jewish officials they returned to their company, and they all "lifted up their voice to God with one accord" in prayer (Acts 4:23-31). Later, when James was killed and Peter was imprisoned "prayer was made earnestly of the church unto God for him" (Acts

12:1-5). That same night, Peter came to Mary's house "where many were gathered together and were praying" (Acts 12:12).

When Luke's history of the church in Acts begins to center around the activities of Paul there are also some references to Paul's practice of prayer. We see that Paul was a man of prayer in times of difficulty (Acts 16:25), but he also prayed when he parted company with fellow-Christians (Acts 20:36; 21:5), when he was in the temple (Acts 22:17), and when he laid hands on the father of Publius to heal him (Acts 28:7-10). When Paul and Barnabas were sent out from the church in Antioch on the first journey, they fasted and prayed and laid hands on them (Acts 13:1-3). As these two men returned from this journey, they appointed elders in every city and "prayed with fasting" and "commended them to the Lord, on whom they had believed" (Acts 14:23). Both Paul (Acts 27:33-38) and the Lord (Mk. 8:6; Jn. 6:11, 23) are reported to have given thanks for their food.

These examples from the gospels and the book of Acts are enough to establish the fact that Jesus, the apostles, and the early church viewed every incident in life as an event to be dealt with in prayer. They prayed "always" and "without ceasing". If the church of our day could come to believe and practice prayer as the church in the first century did it no doubt would find the same joy of service, share the same triumphant attitude and experience the same kind of results that those godly and zealous Christians knew. May the Lord hasten that day.

> The world has lost the right to prayer,
> And saints have failed to pray;
> What loss sustained beyond repair!
> How blind of heart are they!
>
> The Father speaketh in His word
> He talks no other way!
> And to converse with Him, our Lord,
> We must take time to pray!
>
> There is no trial, grief, or pain,
> No moment of the day,
> But that we may in Jesus' name
> Incline our souls and pray!
>
> Pray in the morning,
> Pray at the noontime,
> Pray in the evening,
> Pray anytime.
>
> Pray when you're happy,
> Pray when in sorrow,
> Pray when you're tempted,
> Pray all the time.

QUESTIONS FOR JOY AND PROFIT

1. What was central in the lives of Bible characters who had their hearts set on God? What evidence do we have on this point?
2. Fill in the required information below:

PASSAGE	PERSON(S)	THING PRAYED
Dan. 9:1-19		
Ex. 32:9-14, 31-32		
1 Sam. 1:1-18		
Gen. 18:9-33		
Matt. 26:36-46		
Psa. 51		
Eph. 3:14-21		
Gen. 32:22-32		

3. In addition to learning about prayer, what is one of the key elements in learning how to pray?
4. What two things about prayer are taught in Luke 18:2-8?

5. How may one pray at "all seasons"?
6. How is prayer related to the other injunctions in Rom. 12:12?
7. What does Paul say about prayer in Col. 4:2?
8. How did Paul pray "night and day" for the Thessalonians?
9. How are Christians to pray "without ceasing"? Does this speak merely of an attitude of prayer being maintained, or is more involved?
10. How did Paul pray "without ceasing" for the Thessalonians?
11. Give some examples of how Jesus prayed before the great events of His life.
12. What did Jesus pray about in the following passages: Lk. 22: 32; Jn. 11 :41; Mk. 6:41; Jn. 12:27-28; Lk. 23:46.
13. Name some instances when Peter was engaged in prayer.
14. Does Acts 12:1-5 refer to individual prayer or prayer offered by a group of Christians? For what was the prayer being offered?
15. Would the manner in which this prayer is offered to God be like the prayer referred to in 1 Cor. 14:14-17? What in this passage shows that this prayer was being lead by someone?

16. Is Acts 4:23-31 an example of individual or corporate prayer?
17. Give the passage of Scripture that reports the following things about prayers offered to God by Paul:

    ___Gave thanks for food

    ___Offered in jail

    ___Upon departing from the Ephesian elders

    ___In connection with a healing

    ___In the temple

    ___Upon leaving Tyre

18. Who wrote the song, "Pray All the Time," quoted at the end of this lesson? Who wrote the music? What is the meaning of the first line, "The world has lost the right to pray, And saints have failed to pray"?
19. How does the chorus in this song define the meaning of praying "always" and "without ceasing"?

7

The Qualities of Prayer (I)

A good understanding of the characteristics, conditions and the content of prayer is vitally important for successful communion with God through prayer. One may pray without this understanding, but he cannot pray acceptably without an awareness of the divine laws that govern prayer and make it acceptable to God. Even though we do not find all spelled out for us on any one page in our New Testament a convenient list of the things to do and not to do in prayer, we can by taking into account all that the Bible does have to say about prayer come to know what does please God and what does not please Him. Some things may prove to be of little consequence while others will be absolutely essential. In this chapter and the one to follow we are concerned with what should characterize our prayers to God.

PRAY ON YOUR HEAD

In the Bible we see that David praised God (a likely reference to prayer) seven times a day (Ps. 119:164), probably at stated times in the day (See Ps. 55:17; cf. Acts 10:30). Daniel was accustomed to pray three times a day (Dan. 6: 10). People prayed kneeling (1 Kgs. 8:54; Ezra 9:5; Acts 7:60; 20:36), standing (1 Sam. 1:26; 1 Kgs. 8:14, 22; Neh. 9:4; Mk. 11:25. Lk. 18:11, 13), sitting (2 Sam. 7:18), or even lying prostrate (Matt. 26:39). They prayed sometimes with hands uplifted (1 Kgs. 8:22; Ps. 28:2; 134:2; 1 Tim. 2:8); sometimes beating on their breasts (Lk. 18: 13); sometimes eyes lifted up to heaven (Jn. 11:41); sometimes head bowed (Lk. 18:13). People prayed silently (1 Sam. 1:13), and they prayed aloud (Ezek. 11:13; Jn. 11:41-42; 1 Cor. 14:16); they prayed alone (Mk. 1:35; Matt. 6:6), and they prayed together (Ps. 35:18; Acts 4:31); they prayed in bed (Ps. 63:6), in the open field (Gen. 24:11-12), in the temple (2 Kgs. 19:14; Acts 22:17), at the riverside (Acts 16:13), on the

THE QUALITIES OF PRAYER (I)

seashore (Acts 21 : 5), on the battlefield (I Sam. 7:5), on the housetop (Acts 10 :9), in the house (Acts 10:30), or in jail (Acts 16:25).

A quick glance at this list of references to prayer makes it obvious that many of the things that characterize our prayers have little if any significance at all. None of the things listed here is given any special treatment anywhere in the New Testament, except of course certain restrictions are placed on women in the public worship (1 Cor. 14:34-35). Prayer may be engaged in at any place, at any time, in any posture. In fact, any place, any time, any posture, and any circumstance may very well prove to be the best place, time, posture and circumstance for prayer. The poem, "The Prayer of Cyrus Brown," by Sam Walter Foss, well illustrates this point:

> "The proper way for man to pray,"
> Said Deacon Lemuel Keyes,
> "And the only proper attitude,
> Is down upon his knees."
>
> "No, I should say the way to pray,"
> Said Reverend Doctor Wise,
> "Is standing straight with outstretched arms
> And rapt and upturned eyes."
>
> "Oh, no no, no," said Elder Slow,
> "Such posture is too proud,

> A man should pray with eyes fast-closed
> And head contritely bowed."
>
> "It seems to me his hands should be
> Austerely clasped in front
> With both thumbs pointing toward the ground," Said
> Reverend Doctor Blunt.
>
> "Last year I fell in Hidgeskin's well
> Headfirst," said Cyrus Brown,
> "With both my heels a-stickin' up
> And my head a-pointin' down.
>
> "And I made a prayer right then and there,
> The best prayer I ever prayed,
> The prayingest prayer I ever prayed,
> A-standin' on my head."

One thing that stands out above all others on the characteristics of prayer is this: we should live so close to God, so filled with adoration and reverence for Him, that our spirit is always one of thankfulness and our desire is ever one of concern for one another as brethren. When Christians are so wholly wrapped-up in God, and in the brethren and their welfare and faithfulness and progress, this spirit of conscious dependence on God and concern for others will naturally overflow into uttered prayer in an unceasing manner. The words of Leon Morris (commenting on 1 Thess. 5:17) seem to me to get to the heart of the matter:

THE QUALITIES OF PRAYER (I)

> It is instructive to read again and again in Paul's letters the many prayers that he interjects. Prayer was as natural to Paul as breathing. At any time he was likely to break off his argument or to sum it up by some prayer of greater or less length. In the same way our lives can be lived in such an attitude of dependence on God that we will easily and naturally move into the words of prayer on all sorts of occasions, great and small, grave and gay. Prayer is to be constant.

SPECIFIC QUALITIES THAT MATTER

In addition to this general quality of closeness to God and one another there are certain specific qualities that must characterize prayer. These are the things that really count, not such externals as time, place, occasion or posture. This does not mean that no attention should be given to externals. Certainly one occasion may be more conducive to prayer than another. A certain posture such as kneeling in prayer may seem more appropriate on some occasions (such as occasions of great solemnity or distress) than on others. This is also true of such other factors as time and place. Each Christian must make such judgments for himself. God has not established a rigid formulae for us when it comes to prayer, and we certainly should not take it on ourselves to do that for others. Let us now take a look at some of the qualities of prayer that do matter with God.

1. Humility. Humility is a quality of life that should characterize our every thought and activity. It is often stressed in Scripture as the central ingredient for success, and pride, its opposite, is the cause of failure. Pride takes on many forms, as Robert J. McCracken shows us:

> It attaches itself to and poisons every pursuit and activity of mankind. Pride of rank—the delight taken in status, recognition, honors, in being at the head of the table, the top of the line, the cynosure of all eyes. Pride of intellect—the arrogance that thinks it knows more than it does, forgets the finiteness of the human mind, talks in terms of morons, smiles at the cultural crudity of contemporaries, and needs to be told what Madame Foch said to one of her sons who was boasting about a school prize: 'Cleverness which has to be mentioned does not exist.' Pride of power—the passion to achieve it, to wield more and more of it, to feel superior to others, to give orders with a strident voice and move men like pawns on a chessboard. Pride of nation—shot through with pretension and deception, resulting in the deification of the national interest, in definitions of good and evil which have little relation to uni-

The Qualities of Prayer (I)

> versal moral law, in the egotism of the will-to-power asserting itself as a disinterested activity, ...

The book of Proverbs says pride leads to destruction (16:18), brings one low (29:23), and leads to contention (13:10) and shame (11:2). Humility will help one find both honor (29:23) and wisdom (11:2).

James links humility with prayer. He quotes from the Old Testament which says, "God resisteth the proud, but giveth grace to the humble" (4:6), and then follows the quotation with an exhortation, "Humble yourselves in the sight of the Lord, and he shall exalt you" (4:10). Humility is essential to drawing near to God (4:8) and submitting to Him (4:7). Without it prayer that pleases God and gets the desired results is impossible: "... ye have not, because ye ask not. Ye ask, and receive not, because ye ask amiss, that ye may spend it on your pleasures" (4:2b-3).

Jesus also teaches an important lesson on the necessity of humility in prayer in the parable of the Pharisee and the publican (Lk. 18:9-14). When one reads the prayers of these two men and pays close attention to how they conducted themselves, it is clear that the contrast between them is a contrast between pride and humility. The difference is between self-exaltation and self-humiliation, between a feeling of excellence in religious attainment and a feeling of unworthiness due to a deep sense of guilt as a sinner before God, between self-glorification and shame of sin committed against God. The lesson to be gained from the parable is that for prayer to be accepted by God it must be characterized by humility. The hallmark of false prayer is self-exaltation. The mark of true prayer is a heart completely emptied of self-reliance.

> The world, I thought, belonged to me
> Goods, gold, and people, land and sea
> Where'er I walked beneath God's sky,
> In those old days, my word was "I."
>
> Years passed: there flashed my pathway near
> The fragment of a vision dear;
> My former word no more sufficed,
> And what I said was—"I and Christ."
>
> But, O, the more I looked on Him
> His glory grew, while mine grew dim;
> I shrank so small, he towered so high,
> All I dared say was—"Christ and I."
>
> Years more the vision held its place
> And looked me steadily in the face;
> I speak now in a humbler tone,
> And what I say is—"Christ alone."

THE QUALITIES OF PRAYER (I)

QUESTIONS FOR JOY AND PROFIT

1. From the references cited in this lesson, what was David's practice of prayer?
2. Did Peter likely pray at stated times? See if you can find what Jewish practice was in Jesus' day.
3. Name some people named in the Bible as sometimes kneeling when they prayed. Must one always kneel when he prays? Are there occasions that might be more appropriate for kneeling than others?
4. What was a common custom when praying according to 1 Tim. 2:8? Does this set a binding pattern for us today? Compare this with Rom. 16:16. What descriptive word is common to both customs named in these two verses? Does this remove the emphasis away from the form of the custom itself to the spirit behind the form?
5. Must one always pray aloud?
6. May one offer a prayer in a public place without bowing his head and closing his eyes?
7. Name some places where people prayed, according to the Bible.

8. What one thing is required above all else before one can practice praying unceasingly?
9. How does Leon Morris explain how Paul could pray in an unceasing manner?
10. What is humility? Pride?
11. What are some of the forms pride takes, according to the description of Robert J. McCracken?
12. What does pride do for one? Humility?
13. What does James say is essential to draw near to God? Why?
14. What is the primary point in the parable of the Pharisee and publican?
15. What points in the prayer of the Pharisee show he is self-centered and proud?
16. What does the beating on the breast tell us about the publican?
17. Does the fact that the Pharisee was standing tell us anything about him?
18. What is the point about the publican "standing afar off"?
19. How does the poem at the end of the lesson address the subject of pride and humility?

8

The Qualities of Prayer (II)

In continuing our study of the qualities of prayer we should keep in mind that we are talking about things that are to be viewed seriously because it is these things that make prayer true rather than false prayer. If our prayers are not characterized by these qualities they are not pleasing to God. In our last lesson we considered the importance of humility in prayer. We now take up some other important qualities that must characterize our prayers.

2. Love. The second essential quality of prayer is love. Like humility, love is always admirable, and both pride, the opposite of humility, and hate, the opposite of love, are despised by both God and man. Love is not easily defined. It is best understood in terms of what it does.

When Paul discussed the subject of love in 1 Corinthians 13 he gave a description of love rather than a definition. He described what it does, not what it means. When the Bible talks about love in connection with prayer it does the same thing. It considers love and prayer in terms of what love does.

In the Sermon on the Mount Jesus taught us to pray that God will forgive us of our trespasses, but only as we also have forgiven our debtors (Matt. 6:12). God's love must echo in us in concrete ways before we can realize the benefits of His love in us. If we are not forgiving of those who have wronged us we have no right to expect God to forgive us of our sins (Matt. 6:14-15). Mercy is given only to those who show mercy to others (Jas. 2:13). Jesus said on another occasion, "And whensoever ye stand praying, forgive, if ye have aught against anyone; that your father also who is in heaven may forgive you your trespasses" (Matt. 11:25).

> Only, O Lord, in Thy dear love
> Fit us for perfect rest above;
> And help us this and every day
> To live more nearly as we pray.

The Qualities of Prayer (II)

This lesson on forgiveness and prayer is more fully illustrated in the parable of the unmerciful servant (Matt. 18:21-35). The question of whether man ought to forgive one who has wronged him is not raised. The question raised and answered in the parable is whether there is a limit to forgiveness. Peter knew one must forgive his fellowman, but what if he constantly falls into the same sin? Peter seems to be quite liberal in his feelings about how many times one should be willing to forgive in such a case as that, because he asks, "Until seven times?" But Jesus' reply, "Until seventy times seven" (or, the word may mean merely seventy-seven times, since the Greek phrase is obscure), shows that there is to be no limit set on forgiveness. As God's mercy is unlimited, so we too must show unlimited mercy toward those who wrong us. This is the central point illustrated by the parable which follows.

The sum of money that the servant owed the king was in the millions of dollars, an amount he could never begin to pay, even though he promised to pay all he owed! When he threw himself on the mercy of the king, the king showed pity and canceled the debt altogether. But, alas! the servant who had been shown such incredible kindness immediately showed a mean and unforgiving spirit toward one of his own servants who owed him a minimal amount. The king's response to this unmerciful servant was, "Thou wicked servant, I forgave thee all that debt, because thou besoughtest me: shouldest not thou also have had mercy on thy fellow servant, even as I" (Matt. 18:32-33). In his anger the king turned the servant over to the tormentors. The lesson of the parable is: "So shall also my heavenly Father do unto you, if ye forgive not everyone his brother from your hearts" (Matt. 18:35).

For one to pray for forgiveness, as this servant did, and yet be unforgiving himself as he was, makes one's request to God a farce, or futile, to say the least. One with this kind of mean spirit has surely failed to grasp the meaning of the great love of God in his own life. Apart from knowing that love, one cannot love his fellowman as he ought.

> Could we with ink the ocean fill
>   Were the whole world with parchment made,
> Were every single stick a quill,
>   Were every man a scribe by trade;
>
> To write the love of God alone
>   Would drain the ocean dry;
> Nor could the scroll contain the whole
>   Though stretched from sky to sky.

THE QUALITIES OF PRAYER (II)

3. Expectancy. Another quality of true prayer is expecting God to look favorably upon our requests. On one occasion the disciples were unable to cast a demon out of a young boy, and in disappointment they came to Jesus and asked, "Why could not we cast it out?" (Matt. 17:19). Jesus answered, "Because of your little faith: for verily I say unto you, If ye have faith as a grain of mustard seed, ye shall say unto this mountain, 'Remove thence to yonder place'; and it shall remove; and nothing shall be impossible unto you" (Matt 17:20-21).

Jesus Himself was not in the habit of relocating mountains, so it is not likely that His response was to be taken literally. A rabbi who could remove noted difficulties of interpretation was spoken of as "a remover of mountains." In Scripture removing mountains was a proverbial statement for overcoming difficulties (Is. 40:4; 49:11; 54:10). If the statement of Jesus is to be taken in this sense, the meaning is that what is impossible with men may be accomplished through faith in the power of God.

In Mark 11:22-23 we read where Jesus used this same illustration in a conversation with Peter to explain how He was able to cause a fig tree to stop bearing fruit. Here however Jesus added this significant note: "... and shall not doubt in his heart, but shall believe that what he saith cometh to pass; he shall have it. Therefore I say unto you, All things whatsoever ye pray and ask for, believe that ye receive them, and ye shall have them" (Mk. 11:23b-24). The first part of this statement emphasizes the reality of and need for genuine faith in prayer. If one questions in his heart whether God will in fact grant his needs he has in fact made it impossible for God to grant them. James uses almost identical language when he tells us to pray "in faith, nothing doubting," when we pray for wisdom (Jas. 1:6). Doubt is the sure sign that one's mind is in dispute with itself. When this state of mind exists, James says such a double-minded person should not "think that he will receive anything of the Lord" (Jas. 1:7).

The faith called for in these passages is not a mere creedal statement. It is the conviction and assurance that everything is possible with God; that He gives what He promises. This faith is the full persuasion of heart that there is no burden so heavy that God will not help us to carry it, and there is no problem so insoluble that He will not help us resolve it.

THE QUALITIES OF PRAYER (II)

All things are possible in believing prayer! Not in the sense that God will do for us according to our fanciful notions, or that He will work miracles today in answer to our prayers. But the Christian must pray in full assurance that God will answer his prayers in a way that will be best for him, even though it may prove to be in a way he least expected, and perhaps even in a way he will not fully understand.

> O God of the impossible!
>   Since all things are of Thee
> But soil in which Omnipotence
>   Can work almightily,
>
> Each trial may to us become
>   The means that will display
> How o're what seems impossible
>   Our God hath perfect sway!
>
> The little storms that beat upon
>   Our little barque so frail,
> But manifest Thy power to quell
>   All forces that assail.
>
> The things that are to us too hard,
>   The foes that are too strong,
> Are just the very ones that may
>   Awake a triumph song.
>
> O God of the Impossible,
>   When we no hope can see,
> Grant us the faith that still believes
>   ALL possible to Thee!

4. Watchfulness. In Matthew 26 we are told that Jesus left Peter, James and John behind and went aside alone to pray. Before departing however he charged them, "Abide ye here, and watch with me" (Matt. 26:38). After a brief separation, He returned and found them sleeping. He said to Peter, "What, could ye not watch with me one hour? Watch and pray, that ye enter not into temptation: the spirit indeed is willing, but the flesh is weak" (Matt. 26:41). The following verses tell us that Jesus left them two more times and prayed the same words each time. When he returned to them all three times He found them sleeping. In this passage sleeping contrasts with watchfulness. The admonition to watch is given many times in Scripture, and it is often linked with prayer (Mk. 13:33; Lk. 21:36; Eph. 6:18; Col. 4:2).

Watchfulness in prayer is needed to always be ready for the Lord's return (Mk. 13:33) and to guard against temptation (Matt. 26:41). Slothfulness in this regard breeds weakness due to the flesh and must be intensely guarded against. When we fail to watch in prayer our mental and spiritual alertness is impaired, and we become more susceptible to being overcome by temptation. As James G. S.

S. Thomson puts it, in this situation "outward circumstances and inward weaknesses conspire to become occasions for sin."

Peter admonishes us, "Be sober, be watchful: your adversary the devil, as a roaring lion, walketh about, seeking whom he may devour: whom withstand steadfast in your faith, knowing that the same sufferings are accomplished in your brethren who are in the world" (1 Pet. 5:8-9). "Withstand steadfast in your faith"!! Faith is implicit in watchfulness during prayer. We have already considered the important place of faith in prayer in an earlier section. When such faith is joined in watchfulness in prayer, then we see more clearly how "this is the victory that hath overcome the world, even our faith" (1 Jn. 5:4).

> Christian, seek not yet repose,
>   Cast thy dreams of ease away;
> Thou art in the midst of foes;
>   Watch and pray.
>
> Gird thy heavenly armor on,
>   Wear it every night and day;
> Near thee lurks the evil one;
>   Watch and pray.
>
> Hear the victors who o'ercame;
>   Still they watch each warrior's way;
> And with one deep voice exclaim,
>   "Watch and pray."

QUESTIONS FOR JOY AND PROFIT

1. Is there such a thing as true vs false prayer? In light of our present study how may prayer be false?
2. What is love?
3. What is the second greatest commandment in the law? What is the first?
4. How does love behave according to Paul's description in 1 Cor. 13? Do you see anything that would touch on the subject of forgiveness in his description?
5. In the Sermon on the Mount how does Jesus show we ought to love one another? How does this relate to prayer?
6. What does James say on this subject? What does "mercy glorieth against judgment" mean?
7. Does Mk. 11:25 say the same thing on this subject?
8. Does verse 26 make forgiveness a condition for receiving forgiveness from God?
9. What is the central lesson in the parable of the unmerciful servant? Does this parable address the subject of prayer? How?

The Qualities of Prayer (II)

10. What was the most outstanding inconsistency in the behavior of the unmerciful servant?
11. Is the statement by Jesus about "removing a mountain" always to be understood in a literal way in other passages? If it is not literal in Matt. 17:20-21, what might it mean? If literal, how would the promise be limited?
12. How inclusive is "all things" in Mk. 11:23b-24?
13. If a person doubts when he prays should he expect anything from God? Why?
14. How does the poem at the end of the first section treat the "all things" of Mk. 11:25-26? Do you agree?
15. What two reasons does Jesus give for watching in prayer?
16. What is impaired when we fail to watch? What then is the result?
17. What does Jesus mean when He says, "the spirit indeed is willing, but the flesh is weak"? What is "the flesh" in this statement? Does it refer to literal flesh or to something else?
18. What reason does Peter give for watching?
19. What are some passages from Paul that link watchfulness with prayer?

20. How important is faith in watchfulness in prayer?
21. Write beside the passages below other qualities that should characterize our prayers which have not been discussed in these two chapters:

Lk. 11: 5-8

Lk. 18: 1-8

Matt. 6:5ff.

9

The Conditions of Acceptable Prayer

Prayer and the terms upon which God has promised to answer prayer have not been established by man. The universe was not created by man, nor is it under man's control. The fact that God created both man and the world in which he lives argues for God's right to reveal to man the terms upon which prayer is to be answered. God has not promised to give us "just anything", nor has He left us to bring our petitions to Him in just any way we wish. There are conditions to be met if prayer is to be acceptable to Him.

A careful study of the context of the passages where Jesus promises to give "whatsoever ye shall ask" will reveal that certain conditions are stated, and the promise rests upon these conditions. We will now look at two of these conditions, and then we will give some consideration to godly living and how it relates to these conditions.

IN THE NAME OF CHRIST

When Jesus promised His disciples that He would do whatever they asked, He based His promise upon this important condition: "And whatsoever ye shall ask in my name, that will I do, that the Father may be glorified in the Son. If ye shall ask anything in my name, that will I do" (Jn. 14:13-14). This promise is repeated just a short while later, including the special condition that the prayer be offered to the Father "in my name" (Jn. 15:15). Then, again in John 16:23-24 the promise and condition are given, and for the first time we are specifically told that this is a new stipulation: "Hitherto have ye asked nothing in my name, ..." We will consider why this new requirement was not introduced before this time a little later, but first we need to look into the meaning of praying in the name of Christ.

The meaning of this condition has been a subject of much discussion. We will here give a

The Conditions of Acceptable Prayer

summary of the different ways in which the terms "in the name of Christ" have been defined.

1. As Christ's representative. Some feel that "in the name of Christ" means praying and working as Christ's representatives. To do these things as Christ would do them, and thus as His representatives, would mean that we are to pray and work in the same spirit in which Christ prayed and worked, especially in the spirit of total surrender to the will of God— "Not My will, but Thine be done."

Some parallels to this kind of use of "in the name of" would be found in Matthew 10:41-42 where "in the name of" is used in reference to "a prophet", "a righteous man", and "a disciple". In this passage "in the name of" means to receive the prophet "as a prophet", to receive a righteous man "as a righteous man", and to receive a disciple "as a disciple". But this is seen by some as meaning the same as to receive them as Christ's representatives. Even a better example seems to appear in Matthew 18:5 where Jesus said that the person who receives a little child "in Christ's name" is to receive the child as belonging to Christ, or as Christ's representative. See also Mark 9:41.

W. L. Walker applies this meaning to praying "in the name of Christ" in this way:

> To pray in the name of Jesus, to ask anything in His name, according to His promises, ... is not merely to add to our prayers (as is so often unthinkingly done), 'we ask all in the name of Jesus,' or 'through Jesus Christ our Lord,' etc.; but to pray or ask, as His representatives on earth, in His mission and stead, in His Spirit and with His aim, it implies union with Christ and abiding in Him, He in us and we in Him. The meaning of the phrase is, 'as being one with me, even as I am revealed to you.' Its two correlatives are 'in me,' and the Pauline 'in Christ'".

James G. S. S. Thomson shows what it means to pray as Christ's representative:

> An ambassador exercises his authority in the name of his sovereign only because he submits to his sovereign's will, and acts as his sovereign's representative. So to pray in Christ's name is to pray as Christ would pray; and surely He has taught us that the true aim of prayer is complete submission to the Father's will, that He may do His will for us, in us, and through us.

2. Faith in Christ's Revelation of Himself.
This view says that prayer in the name of Christ is a prayer that is in harmony with whatever Christ has revealed concerning Himself. Christ's name denotes the revelation by which we know Jesus. This revelation which is referred to by the word "name" in relation to Christ covers His person as well as His work. His person and work are best seen, or revealed to us, in the titles which are attributed to Christ. The self-revelation referred to by Christ's "name" is limited to the sphere of redemption, and therefore in the passages which require praying in Christ's name a definite limit as to what may be prayed for is seen to exist. R. C. H. Lenski, who holds this view, thinks the word "in" in relation to "name" places this limit on the requests that may be made:

> And *en* has its natural sense of sphere: 'in union with,' 'in connection with.' This *en* draws a circle around the action of asking, the boundary is the *onoma* (name, *ww*). Hence not 'on the basis of my name,' 'through my name,' which would change the preposition. To pray in Jesus' name naturally involves faith in the revelation, also that the petition abide in the circle of that revelation.

Some prayers would not be in harmony with what Jesus reveals about Himself and could not therefore be "in the name of Christ". One could not, for example, pray out of his own selfish desires, aims and ambitions. One could not pray for personal revenge, out of personal ambition or out of a desire to surpass someone else "in the name of Christ".

3. In Acknowledgement of All That the Name Implies. Another possible meaning of these terms, and a view that is often expressed, is that "in the name of Christ" means prayer should be offered in accord with all that the name stands for, such as authority, character, rank, majesty, power, excellence, etc. Henry Thayer says it means "... relying or resting on the name of Christ, rooted (so to speak) in his name, i.e., mindful of Christ and reliance on the word which invites us to him." Alvah Hovey says, "To ask in the name of Christ, is to ask as a servant of Christ, honoring his authority, trusting in his grace, and seeking to do his will." In the ancient world the name stood for the whole person.

So to do something in one's name was to do it thinking of all that a person's name represented, the whole person, including his character, will and power. To pray "in" the name of Christ is to utter a prayer "proceeding from faith in Christ, prayer that gives expression to a unity with all that Christ stands for, prayer which seeks to set forward Christ Himself," as Leon Morris worded it.

Whichever of these views seems to us to best represent the meaning of prayer in the name of Christ, it must be clear that Jesus is not saying that we must merely attach the words, "In the name of Christ we pray, Amen," to the end of our prayers. How often we must have heard brethren add these words to the end of their prayer as though they were merely repeating a formula which Christ requires that we use at the close of each prayer. Nothing could be farther from the truth. We would not advocate that the name of Christ not be said in our prayers, but we would hope that we will consistently pray "in the name of Christ" by DOING what we SAY when we utter the words, "In the name of Christ we ask these things, Amen."

What did Jesus mean when He said, "Hitherto have ye asked nothing in my name," (Jn. 16:24)? It surely did not mean that the disciples had not prayed in the spirit of Christ prior to this time. They undoubtedly knew a good bit about Christ before the time that Jesus gave this discourse, and they must have prayed in full awareness of the knowledge they possessed up to this time. But their knowledge was limited, and the new dimension of prayer which Jesus now introduced pointed to the new awareness that the disciples would have of Jesus as "a ransom for many" (Matt. 20:28). They would come to see Him as their great high priest and sin offering, as "the Lamb of God, that taketh away the sin of the world!" (Jn. 1:29), and as "a propitiation for our sins, and not for ours only; but also for the whole world" (1 Jn. 2:2). They had known Jesus as a Divine Teacher, the true Messiah, and the Son of the living God, but they had not known Him as the only Mediator between God and man and as their Intercessor before the Father (1 Tim. 2:5; Heb. 7:25).

Prayer from this time forward must be offered to God in full awareness of this all important truth about Jesus. That this is the new thing about Jesus which calls for prayer "in His name" is indicated by the fact that Jesus introduced this new condition on the night before His death, and He gave as the reason for His disciples doing greater works than He had done, "because I go unto the Father." Then immediately He added the promise that He would grant whatever they asked in His name (Jn. 14:12). His going unto the Father not only introduced a period of greater works, but it also introduced a time in which prayer would be offered in His name.

ACCORDING TO HIS WILL

A second condition of acceptable prayer is given by John in his first epistle: "And this is the boldness which we have toward him, that, if we ask anything according to his will, he heareth us: and if we know that he heareth us whatsoever we ask, we know that we have the petitions which we asked of him" (1 Jn. 5:14-15). The "anything" and "whatsoever" of these verses are parallel to the "whatsoever" in the passages we studied in the previous section. Just as there was a condition to pray "in His name" in those verses, the condition in this passage is that we pray "according to his will."

This is the fourth time in this epistle that John has spoken of boldness (ASV) or confidence (KJV). In 2:28 he speaks of boldness in itself—

not being ashamed when in God's presence; in 3:21 boldness is a result of a clear conscience; in 4:17 our boldness in the day of judgment is said to be due to our likeness to Christ, and to the spirit of love we have received because of Him. In this passage John speaks of a result of our boldness: we feel free to approach God, and we feel sure that He hears our petitions. There is however one condition: *we shall not ask what He is not likely to grant.* In fact, John is assuming that the person who has such confidence and who is in such spiritual union as this confidence would require will not make requests that are out of harmony with the Lord's will. The disciple's will is one with the will of His Lord. He desires to receive only what the Lord wills for him and for others. God's will is for our good, and our requests should be offered to God in this awareness.

The prayer of the Christian is the same as that of his Lord, "... nevertheless, not my will, but thine, be done" (Lk. 22:42). James (4:3) shows that some petitions are not answered with a "yes" from the Lord because we wish to spend what we receive on our own pleasures. This kind of prayer is not "according to his will." John himself goes ahead and shows that he is thinking especially of prayer for an erring brother (5:16-17). It would not be "according to his will" to pray for one who has committed a "sin unto death." In our next lesson we will study the kinds of things we are to pray for, both for ourselves and for others.

GODLY LIVING

One thing that has been seen to lie behind the two conditions of acceptable prayer we have studied in this lesson has been a quality of life that reflects a close relationship with God. Submission to God was central to all the views we presented on the meaning of praying in the name of Christ. Praying in the name of Christ implies union with Christ and abiding in Him. The same may be said for praying according to His will. This implies that the Christian is one with Christ, that he abides in Christ and Christ abides in him. Jesus taught His disciples that such abiding is essential if we are to ask "whatsoever ye will" with the expectation that "it shall be done unto you" (Jn. 15:7).

James says that the prayer that avails is the prayer of a "righteous" man (Jas. 5:16b). Peter says, "The eyes of the Lord are upon the righteous, and his ears unto their supplication: But the face of the Lord is against them that do evil" (1 Pet. 3:12). The statement of the man whom Jesus healed of his blindness affirms the same thing: "We know that God heareth not sinners: but if any man be a worshiper of God, and do his will, him he heareth" (Jn. 9:31). God hears the prayers of those who are obedient to Him (Ps. 18:41; 66:18; Prov. 1:28; 15:29; Is. 1:15). John says, "Beloved, if our heart condemn us not, we have boldness toward God; and whatsoever we ask we receive of him, because we keep his commandments and do the things that are pleasing in his sight" (1 Jn. 3:21-22).

> Art Thou not weary of our selfish prayers,
>   Forever crying, "Help me! Save me, Lord."
> We stay fenced in by petty fears and cares,
>   Nor hear the song outside, nor join its vast accord.
>
> Is not the need of others souls our need?
>   After desire, the helpful act must go,
> As the strong wind bears on the winged seed
>   To some bare spot of earth, and leaves it there to grow.
>
> Still are we saying, "Teach us how to pray!"
>   Oh, teach us how to love, and then our prayer
> Through other lives will find its upward way,
>   As plants together seek and find sweet light and air.

QUESTIONS FOR JOY AND PROFIT

1. Who is the only one who has the right to give the conditions upon which prayer will be answered? Why?
2. Does praying in the name of Christ mean only that we are to pray "by the authority of Christ"?
3. What passages of Scripture reveal the condition of praying in Christ's name?
4. What is the meaning of Matthew 10:41-42?
5. What is the meaning of Matthew 18:5?
6. What is the meaning of Mark 9:41?
7. How is each of these passages used to illustrate the meaning of praying in the name of Christ?
8. What is the central point made in the quotations from W. L. Walker and James G. S. S. Thomson? What does Walker say about the terms "in Christ" used so frequently by Paul?
9. Explain the view that in the name of Christ refers to the revelation of Christ about Himself.
10. How does Lenski explain the preposition "in" in the phrase "in the name of Christ"?
11. How is the phrase explained by those who believe it refers to all that Christ's name implies?

12. Must one SAY in his prayers, "In the name of Christ we pray" before he has actually prayed in Jesus' name?
13. How was praying in the name of Christ a new requirement?
14. What does it mean to pray "according to his will"?
15. How does the confidence or boldness mentioned by John relate to praying "according to his will"?
16. What kind of prayer according to James would not be according to God's will?
17. How does godly living relate to the two conditions of acceptable prayer we have studied in this lesson?
18. What are some passages of Scripture that tell what kind of person one must be before God will hear his prayer?
19. Who is the person called "the sinner" in John 9:31? Is this the alien sinner? Cf. Cornelius, Acts 10:1-4, 31.
20. Why might God become weary of our prayers according to the author of the poem at the end of the lesson?

10

The Content of Prayer

The Bible has very little to say about what God's people are not to pray for. In addition to the case where John says we are not to pray for the brother who has sinned a sin "unto death", which we have noted in passing, Jeremiah was told, "Therefore pray not thou for this people, neither lift up cry nor prayer for them, neither make intercession to me: for I will not hear thee" (Jer. 7:16). Apart from a few references like this nothing is said about prayer on the negative side. The examples that fall into this class emphasize that prayer is of no value unless it is accompanied by repentance, sincerity, unselfishness, and a knowledge of what is being asked.

Paul says, "In everything by prayer and supplication with thanksgiving let your requests be made known to God" (Phil. 4:6). Every situation is to be viewed by us as an occasion for prayer, not necessarily that we are to pray for "just anything." The New Testament furnishes many examples that serve as a safe guide on the kinds of things we may pray for when we go before the throne of God with our prayer and supplication with thanksgiving. We will look at some things we are to pray *for*, both for others and ourselves.

PRAYING FOR OTHERS

1. Pray for Enemies. In the Sermon on the Mount Jesus said, "Ye have heard that it was said, Thou shalt love thy neighbor, and hate thine enemy: but I say unto you, Love your enemies, and pray for them that persecute you" (Matt. 5:43-44). We may at times feel it is impossible to love those who do us harm, but Jesus gives us no option. He knows it is possible, and not only is it possible, but it is best. No one can lay claim to having attained unto the higher quality of righteousness which Jesus reveals to us in this sermon while hating his enemies. Jesus not only pointed us to the right way here, but He leads us into this better way of life if we will but follow Him. He showed us His love for His enemies by praying for them (Lk. 23:34), and He now says to us, "Come, follow me" (1 Pet. 2:23).

2. Pray for Rulers. Paul says we should "pray for all men; for kings and all that are in high places; that we may lead a tranquil and quiet life in all godliness and gravity" (1 Tim. 2:1-2). The "all men" would include enemies, even rulers who might be antagonistic to the cause of Christ. Christians are to be subject to those who govern because they are appointed by God to protect the innocent and punish evil doers (Rom. 13:1-7; 1 Pet. 2:13-17). God must be involved in such worldly affairs or it would be meaningless to pray with regard to them. It is in the best interest of Christians and the cause which they espouse that world conditions be conducive to living a "quiet and peaceable life, godly and respectful in every way" (RSV). Prayer can help make this possible.

3. Pray for the Salvation of Others. Jesus prayed that God would forgive those who were crucifying Him (Lk. 23:34). This should not be interpreted in such a way as to make Him word a prayer that would not be "according to his will." God has never saved men in the absence of genuine repentance, and Jesus did not pray here that God would do something that would contradict not only God's revealed will but His own nature as well. Even men are expected always to have a willingness to forgive, but the bestowal of forgiveness is contingent upon repentance (Lk. 17:3). Paul said that God would have all men to be saved (1 Tim. 2:4), but not unconditionally. He also wills that all men come to repentance (2 Pet. 3:9), which means that salvation is conditional on man's part (Heb. 5:7-8; 2 Thess. 1:7-9; Pet. 4:17; Mk. 16:16; Acts 2:38). Paul also prayed for the salvation of his Jewish brethren (Rom. 10:1), but he did not ask that God would save them in their unbelief and disobedience.

4. Pray for Spiritual Growth and the Progress of the Gospel. In Paul's letters we find frequent references to his prayers for his brethren, and oftentimes he called on them to pray for him. The content of these prayers, and requests for prayer on his behalf, most often had to do with the spiritual growth of his fellow-Christians (Phil. 1:9; Col. 1:9; 2 Thess. 1:11; 1 Thess. 5:23; Col. 4:12, etc.), and that he might speak with boldness (Eph. 6:18) and have doors of opportunity opened up to him (Col. 4:3). He asked that the Thessalonians pray for him that "the word of the Lord may have free course" (2 Thess. 3:1). He asked the brethren in Rome to "strive together with me in your prayers to God for me; that I may be delivered from them that are disobedient in Judaea, and that my ministration which I have for Jerusalem may be acceptable to the saints; that I may come to you in joy through the will of God, and together with you find rest" (Rom. 15:30-31). In other words, pray for my deliverance, and pray for my success in the ministry of the gospel, as I pray for you that "the God of peace be with you all, Amen" (Rom. 15:33).

5. Pray for Strength and Forgiveness. Paul prayed that the Ephesians might "be strengthened with power through his Spirit in the inward man; that Christ may dwell in your hearts through faith; ... " (Eph. 3:16-17). Jesus prayed for Peter, "that thy faith fail not," and, He said to Peter, "When once thou hast turned again, establish thy brethren" (Lk. 22:32). A few years later when Simon Peter was strengthening his brethren, another Simon who had recently been converted, but had since sinned against God, asked Peter, "Pray for me to the Lord, that none of these things which you have spoken come upon me" (Acts 8:24). This request came in response to Peter's command to Simon to repent of his wickedness, "and pray the Lord, if perhaps the thought of thy heart shall be forgiven thee" (Acts 8:22). This is what *Christians* are to do when they sin, not what alien sinners who are not yet new creatures in Christ (2 Cor, 5:17) are to do to be saved.

6. Pray for the Sick. In James 5:13-16 we learn that prayer should be offered on behalf of those who are sick. We are first assured that prayer is appropriate in trials of all kinds: "Is any among you suffering? let him pray" (v. 13). The KJV has the word "afflicted" for the word "suffering" in other versions. It is a general word, more general than disease and illness. It is the word used elsewhere to refer to suffering hardship (2 Tim. 2:9; 2:3; 4:5; Jas. 5:10). The sickness mentioned in verse 14 is a specific kind of hardship or suffering. The word "sick" in this verse is used to refer to physical sickness, even though the word literally means "weak," or "to be without strength." This same word is used in Scripture to refer to weaknesses of various kinds, but in this context physical weakness or sickness is referred to by James.

The Content of Prayer

Some brethren have insisted that spiritual sickness is all that James is talking about all the way through this passage. We do not deny that spiritual sickness is introduced, but we do not see that the word "sick" refers to this condition in this passage. The word "sick" in verse 14 refers to physical sickness. But James is not talking about just any sick person. He is talking about that person who is under the burden of bodily suffering who also suffers spiritually, being thereby tempted in his faith. This is why we find running through the passage not only statements about bodily healing, but references to confession and forgiveness of sins as well. It would not seem fitting that James should use the example of Elijah praying for things that involved temporal matters to illustrate the efficacy of prayer for spiritual recovery alone. Illness is a common use of the word (see Mk. 6:5, 6).

The word "save" in verse 15 is also used elsewhere to refer to physical healing (Matt. 9:22; Mk. 5:23; Jn. 11:12, etc.), and this lends support for rendering "heal" in this passage as well. In this verse it means that the sick man will recover. The words "shall raise him up" come from the same Greek word translated "raised up" in Mark 1:31, where Simon Peter's mother-in-law was ***raised up*** from her sick-bed. The raising up had no reference to her cure from her sickness which had already taken place ***before*** she was raised up. The same is true in this passage in James. What we have found is that the cure from the sickness is called to our attention by the word "save", which means heal, and "raise up" refers to raising up from the sick-bed. This means that the reference to "raising up" is an indication that the sickness is physical and not spiritual in nature. If "save" means saved from spiritual sickness, then what would "raise up" refer to? If he has already been "saved" he would not need to be "saved" (raised up) again!

We take the word "healed" in verse 16 also to refer to bodily healing. The reason James has introduced the matter of confession and forgiveness in this passage is that the one who is ill ***and also in sin*** must receive forgiveness lest his sin should stand between him and being healed.

Some who agree that these verses are speaking of bodily healing feel that the language is best understood in terms of miraculous healing. And this view is attractive when we witness so many cases where our prayers seem to have availed nothing in praying for the sick. But might we not also say the same thing about prayers in reference to other things? All we are doing by reasoning in this manner is questioning the validity of prayer for the sick once the age of miracles has ceased. The truth of the matter is, there is nothing in the passage that requires that what James teaches here would apply only at a time when spiritual gifts were possessed.

It is a known fact that oil was used in Bible times for medicinal purposes (Is. 1:6; Lk. 10:34). Why would it be unreasonable to assume that this is the sense in which the use of oil is referred to here in this passage? That elders are instructed to put oil on the body does not present a strong reason for rejecting this view, as some have assumed. The fact that James is requiring that elders oil the body of the sick person for whom they are to pray does not turn them into doctors, nor does it mean that they ought to attempt to give medical advice when they are not qualified to do so. The good Samaritan was no physician, yet he administered oil to a body that needed it (Lk. 10:34). Paul told Timothy to take a little wine for his illness (1 Tim. 5:23). Whatever can be done for one with medicine should be done, "in the name of the Lord." That is, as we have seen in earlier studies, in view of all that Christ's name implies, desiring that the Lord's will be done.

Even though medicinal means are to be used, prayer is the main thing. "The prayer of faith shall save the sick," not the oil. James uses here the kind of words Jesus used when He simply added His great promises to prayer, as we have already witnessed (Matt. 7:7-8; Mk.11:24; Jn. 14:13; 16:23). But just as Jesus added the condition that prayer be offered to God "in His name", so James shows that all of one's life and activities must be lived in acknowledgement of this same condition (Jas. 4:15).

PRAYING FOR OURSELVES

1. Pray for Temporal Needs. In the model prayer for His disciples Jesus teaches that one should pray for his temporal needs. "Bread" in the request, "Give us this day our daily bread," includes the simple necessities of life, such as food, shelter, clothing and health. All things that are needful for the body are meant. Even though our Father knows our needs (Matt. 6:8,

31ff.), we must take the time to ask for them in prayer. We are not to be anxious for our temporal needs. To be anxious implies ignorance of God's providential care (Matt. 6:19-34).

This requirement to pray for temporal needs shows that it is scriptural to pray for material things. But we ought to note that of the six things we are told to pray in this passage only one of them involves physical necessities. Physical needs are not the most important needs, and yet they are a part of our well-being and we are to pray for them. We are to pray for prosperity only to the extent that our soul prospers (3 Jn. 2). We are to pray for our needs one day at a time. For "our daily bread" the ASV footnote reads, "Gr. our bread for the coming day. Or, our needful bread." Prayer is no substitute for work either. We must work and pray (Eph. 4:28; 2 Thess. 3:10; 1 Tim. 5:8), knowing that every good and needful thing comes from God (Jas. 1:17).

2. Pray for Protection from Harm. Jesus also teaches that we should pray for protection from harm, again showing that it is scriptural to pray for physical things. As He warned about the coming destruction of Jerusalem, He said, "And pray ye that your flight b e n ot i n t he winter, neither on a sabbath" (Matt. 24:20). Extreme hardship would have to be endured if their flight from the city was in the winter due to unfavorable travel conditions, and being restricted in travel on the sabbath as the Jews were could jeopardize their lives. Believing that the hand of God is involved in the affairs of this world, Christians should pray for protection even from physical disasters.

3. Pray for Deliverance from Temptation. Jesus teaches us to pray that we will not be led into temptation (Matt. 6:13). Paul assures us that we will not be tempted above what we will be able to withstand (1 Cor. 10:13). In this latter verse Paul says that God provides a way of escape from every temptation.

4. Pray for Forgiveness. Not only are we to pray for one another that we may be forgiven, but we are also to ask God to forgive us of our own sins (Matt. 6:12). God's forgiveness is conditional, not only upon repentance (Acts 8:22), but also upon our forgiveness of those who have wronged us (Matt. 6:12b, 14-15).

5. Pray That the Lord Will Send Forth Laborers. We need to realize that the Lord has sent us forth into His harvest. When Jesus sent

THE CONTENT OF PRAYER

the apostles into the world to preach the gospel, He told them to teach all baptized believers "all things whatsoever I commanded you" (Matt. 28:20). He had commanded them, "Go ye therefore, and make disciples ... baptizing them ... (Matt. 28:19). This means that now we are to do the same. Like one brother has put it, "Go Ye Means Go Me." Jesus said, "Pray ye therefore the Lord of the harvest, that he send forth laborers into his harvest" (Matt. 9:38). If we will begin to pray that the Lord will send forth laborers into His harvest, hopefully we will realize that He is sending each of us to gather His harvest. If not, we ought to stop praying until we start going.

> I asked God for strength, that I might achieve;
> I was made weak, that I might learn humbly to obey.
> I asked for help, that I may do great things;
> I was given infirmities, that I might do greater things.
> I asked for riches, that I might be happy;
> I was given poverty, that I might be wise.
> I asked for power that I might have the praises of men;
> I was given weakness, that I might feel the need of God.
> I asked for all things, that I might enjoy all things.
> I was given life, that I might enjoy all things.
> I got nothing I asked for but everything I hoped for.
> Almost in spite of myself, my unspoken prayers were answered.
> I am among men most richly blessed.

QUESTIONS FOR JOY AND PROFIT

1. Do you see any similarity between what God told Jeremiah not to pray for and what John said not to pray for?
2. Is there a difference in the kind of love one ought to have for his enemies and the kind of love one is to have for God, a husband or wife, etc. Compare *agapao* with *phileo* in John 21:15-17. Which word is used in Matt. 5:44?
3. What should one pray for when he prays for his enemies? What should one do for his enemies? See Rom. 12:18-21.
4. Why should we pray for those in political office?
5. Define the following terms from 1 Tim. 2:2 (ASV). Compare translations.

    Tranquil:

    Quiet:

    Godliness:

    Gravity:

6. Did God forgive all of those who were involved in the crucifixion of Jesus when Jesus prayed that God would forgive them?

7. When were some of those for whom Jesus prayed saved, and on what terms?
8. Is one required to forgive someone who sins against him before he repents?
9. Is it possible to love someone while hating the things he does? Compare how you hate some things you do and how you keep on loving yourself.
10. Write beside the passages below the things Paul prayed for on behalf of other Christians:

    Phil. 1:9-11:

    Col. 1:9-12:

    2 Thess. 1:11-12:

    I Thess. 5:23:

    Col. 4:12 (Epaphras):

    Eph. 3:16-19:

11. What is God able to do according to Eph. 3:20?
12. What example in the Scriptures shows we may pray for forgiveness of sins for someone else? What is such prayer conditioned upon?
13. What is the meaning of the word afflicted

or suffering in Jas. 5:13?
14. What is the meaning of the word "sick" in verse 14?
15. What is the meaning of the word "save" in verse 14?
16. Do the words "sick" and "save" in these verses refer to spiritual or physical sickness?
17. To what does James refer by the words "raise up" in verse 15?
18. Why is confession and forgiveness of sins brought up in these verses?
19. In the promise, "and the prayer of faith shall save him that is sick," does the word "faith" refer to the faith of the elders, of the sick person, or both?
20. Why was oil to be put on the body of the sick person? Does this mean that the practice enjoined in these verses must refer to the exercise of a spiritual gift? If literal oil is meant, would this turn the elders into doctors?
21. Is it scriptural to pray for prosperity? What does the word "bread" mean in Matt. 6:11?
22. Should we expect God to give us our needs if we will not work when we are able?

The Content of Prayer

23. Is it scriptural to pray for physical things according to Jas. 5:17-18; Matt. 6:11; Matt. 24:20? What caution should be given according to Jas. 4:3?
24. Is Matt. 9:38 a prayer that should be prayed for ourselves, or others, or both?
25. What is the main lesson to be learned from the poem at the end of this lesson?
26. Is there ever a time to stop praying for something? See 2 Cor. 12:7-10 and Matt. 20:20-23.

11

Prayer and Salvation

What a privilege it is to go before God in prayer. As the maker of heaven and earth the God of heaven deserves to be adored and worshiped, and mortal man who stands amazed before God yearns for communion with the God "of whom are all things, and we unto him ... and ... through whom are all things, and we through him" (1 Cor. 8:6). In one sense this object of all true worship is the Father of all mankind. The Bible says God is "the Father of spirits" (Heb. 12:9), and that all men are the offspring of God (Acts 17:28).

Every person born into this world is made in the image of God (Gen. 1:26; Jas. 3:9). Man is "but little lower than God" (Ps. 8: 5). This places man in a unique relationship with his Creator. The lower animal creation is not in God's image, nor is it the offspring of God. Man is a creature created for worship because he is capable of looking up into the heavens and observing all of God's magnificent creation, and exclaiming, "How Great Thou Art!" The psalmist exclaims, "The heavens declare the glory of God; And the firmament showeth his handiwork" (Ps. 19:1).

Paul tells us that God manifested Himself to the Gentiles in Old Testament times through His creation, revealing His everlasting power and divinity (Rom. 1:19). Even though they failed to glorify Him as God, and did not give thanks, they should have glorified Him, and they should have given thanks, because God had clearly revealed Himself to them (Rom. 1:20-21). God will hold them accountable for having failed to live up to the knowledge they had. They were without excuse. Only rational creatures, as the very offspring of God, are recognized in Scripture as the sons of God by creation, and because they are so recognized they are accountable before Him as the Father of spirits (Rom. 14:12; 2 Cor. 5:10; Acts 17:30-31; Rev. 20:11-15).

God is also recognized in Scripture as Father in another sense; a more personal and intimate sense. He is the Father of all men by right of creation, but by redemption He is Father in a special but more limited way. He is the Father of all who have been born of the water and the Spirit (Jn. 3:5); all those who are new creatures in Christ (2 Cor. 5:17). One who is in Christ is a child of God by spiritual birth. These are those who are to pray, "Our Father who art in heaven" (Matt. 6:9).

WILL GOD HEAR A SINNER WHEN HE PRAYS?

God will hear any person's prayer who wants to listen to God. He will not hear anyone's prayer, whether a child of God by creation or redemption, who is in rebellion against Him. God's ear is not open to mere words. Jesus said, "Not every one who saith unto me, Lord, Lord, shall enter into the kingdom of heaven; but he that doeth the will of my Father who is in heaven" (Matt. 7:21). Again, "And why call ye me, Lord, Lord, and do not the things which I say?" (Lk. 6:46). The songwriter of the Old Testament said, "If I regard iniquity in my heart, the Lord will not hear" (Ps.

66:18). A wise man said, "He that turneth away his ear from hearing the law, even his prayer is an abomination" (Prov. 28:9). These passages, as well as others (Prov. 15:8, 29; 21:13; Jn. 9:31; 1 Pet. 3:12, etc.), show that God will not hear the prayers of those who are in rebellion against Him.

The Bible claims that all men are sinners: "there is none holy as Jehovah" (1 Sam. 2:2); "there is no man that sinneth not" (1 Kgs. 8:46). Paul says that "all have sinned, and fall short of the glory of God" (Rom. 3:23). Even Christians, children of God by spiritual birth, those who only have the right to cry, "Abba, Father," because they have received the adoption of sons (Gal. 4:5-6; Rom. 8:15), sin against God occasionally (1 Jn. 1:8, 10;2:1-2). Yet, God hears their prayers (Acts 8:22; 1 Jn. 2:1-2). He also heard the prayer of Cornelius, an alien sinner, one who needed words whereby he and his house might be saved (Acts 10:4, 31; 11:14-15). God will hear the prayers of any sinner who is seeking to do the will of God, one who is willing to listen to God and obey His revealed will. The sinner, which the blind man said God will not hear, is the sinner whose heart is set on doing his own will (Jn. 9:31). He is the person who regards iniquity in his heart, or who has turned away his ear from hearing the law.

WILL GOD FORGIVE THE SINS OF THE ALIEN SINNER THROUGH PRAYER?

No. Cornelius is not an example of one who became a child of God, or had his alien sins remitted, through prayer. The Lord told Cornelius that his prayer had been heard, but He then immediately told him, "Send therefore to Joppa, and call unto thee Simon" (Acts 10:32). Why send for Simon? Was it so Simon could tell him he had been saved through prayer? No. Peter later reports it this way: "Send to Joppa, and fetch Simon, whose surname is Peter; who shall speak unto thee words, whereby thou shalt be saved, thou and all thy house" (Acts 11:13-14). Cornelius was not told his prayer had saved him; he was told his prayer had been heard. Here was a man seeking for truth, one who wanted to hear what God would have him do. Cornelius was told to send for Simon Peter who would tell him what to do to be saved.

No person is saved without first being taught (Jn. 6:44-45; Mk. 16:15; Acts 11:14), and no one is saved without obedience to the gospel (2 Thess. 1:8-9; 1 Pet. 4:17; Mk. 16:16; Acts 2:37-38; 22:16). One who is a child of God by physical creation may be honest and sincere, and he may in a sincere way pray to God and have his prayer heard like Cornelius, but Scripture does not teach that he will be saved by his prayer. He will be saved, if he is saved, by "words" just as Cornelius was saved. The gospel is God's power to save (Rom. 1:16).

OTHER CASES EXAMINED

Someone may ask at this point, "But are there not some cases in the New Testament where prayer is said to be the way some people received the remission of sins?" Yes, there are passages which show that repentance and prayer is the way that ***Christians*** who have sinned are to receive forgiveness of sins. Simon of Samaria is an example of one who believed and was baptized (Acts 8:13), and was therefore saved (Acts 8:13 with Mk. 16:15-16), in the same way the other Samaritans were saved (Acts 8:12). When he later sinned ***as a Christia***n he was told to repent and pray that he might be forgiven (Acts 8:22). But there is no case where an alien sinner (one yet outside of Christ, not yet born of water and the Spirit, Jn. 3:3, 5) became a Christian by asking God to forgive him of his sins. Let's take a look at some cases people sometimes bring up in an attempt to prove that prayer is God's way of making Christians.

1. The Prayer of the Publican (Lk. 18:9-14). In an earlier lesson we pointed out that the prayer of the publican illustrates an important quality of prayer. It shows us that acceptable prayer must be characterized by humility. The story contrasts two different attitudes of people under the Jewish dispensation. It does not introduce the subject of how to be initially saved through the gospel of Christ. The right kind of attitude which it upholds is essential to acceptable worship in all ages. Yet both the Pharisee and the Publican lived under the law of Moses at the time Jesus told this story.

The word "justified" in verse 14 is not used in the technical sense in which it later came to be used to describe salvation under the terms of the gospel. Here the word means "approved." As a result of the complete lack of self-assertiveness the publican's worship was approved by God rather than the Pharisee's worship which indicated he was proud of his attainments and loved to be heard and seen by others.

2. The Thief on the Cross (Lk. 23:42-43). The case of the thief on the cross is often used as an example of conversion, but the thief who received mercy upon asking for it of the Lord was not saved upon the terms of the New Covenant ratified by the blood of Christ. Repentance and remission of sins in the name of Christ had not yet begun to be preached. Jesus promised that this would be done "beginning from Jerusalem" (Lk. 24:47). The apostles were not to do this until they had received the "promise of the Father" (Lk. 24:48-49), which would endue them with power by the baptism of the Holy Spirit (Lk. 24:49; Acts 1:4-5). The Holy Spirit would lead them into all truth (Jn. 16:13). The apostles received the Holy Spirit on the day of Pentecost and began to preach salvation in the name of Christ for the first time from Jerusalem, as Jesus had promised (Acts 2:1-4; 2:37-38). Peter later called the events of this day "the beginning" (Acts 11:15).

The terms of pardon in the name of Christ which were preached for the first time on the day of Pentecost did not include prayer (Acts 2:36-

38). Prayer is nowhere preached as a condition of salvation to alien sinners in all of the accounts of conversion recorded in the book of Acts, and yet beginning in Acts 2 we have remission of sins in the name of Christ preached in every city where the gospel was taken under the great commission.

Christ Himself was born under the law (Gal. 4:4). The New Covenant could not become effective until after Christ's death (Heb. 9:16-17). Both covenants could not be in operation at the same time because "He taketh away the first that he may establish the second" (Heb. 10:9). To be joined to both covenants at the same time would be spiritual adultery, just as one is in adultery when he is married to two companions at the same time (Rom. 7:1-4). Christ nailed the Old Testament law to the cross and took it out of the way (Col. 2:14). He abolished the law through His death on the cross (Eph. 2:13-16). Since the thief lived and died under the first covenant, he is not to be used as an example of conversion for those who live under the terms of the second or new covenant.

3. Calling on the Name of the Lord. Peter preached on the day of Pentecost, "Whosoever shall call on the name of the Lord shall be saved" (Acts 2:21), and Paul later affirmed the same thing (Rom. 10:13). Some think this refers to prayer, but does it? Let's see. It is clear that those who asked what they must do to be saved in Acts 2:37 had not understood Peter's statement in verse 21 to mean that the sinner must pray for salvation. If they did understand that to call on the Lord's name in this instance meant prayer, then why did they ask, "What must we do?" in verse 37? If to call meant prayer in v. 21 they would have already known what they must do. It is equally clear that Peter had not himself meant prayer because in his answer to their question he commanded repentance and baptism for the remission of sins (Acts 2:38).

This was Peter's explanation of what it means to call on the Lord's name for salvation. Had Peter meant prayer in verse 21, he would have answered the question of verse 37 in this way: "You already know what to do. I told you to "call on the name of the Lord," and that means you must pray that you might be freed from your sins." Had the people understood verse 21 to mean prayer, they would not have asked the question, "What must we do?" Again, we can be assured that had Peter meant prayer at that place (v. 21), he would not have answered their question with something different in verse 38. To call on the name of the Lord in Acts 2:21 is equal to obeying the gospel as it is revealed by Peter in vv. 36-38.

But what about Paul's reference to calling on the name of the Lord in Romans 10:13-17? Could it possibly refer to prayer? Not if the view that one is saved at the point of faith without any further acts of obedience is true. But this is what is believed by so many people today. Of course this argument is made in an attempt to rule out baptism as a requirement for salvation. But if salvation by faith means baptism is not essential because you cannot have an overt act necessary to salvation following faith, then the argument that "call" in Romans 10:13 means pray cannot be true because prayer also is an overt act like baptism, and in this verse "call" follows faith in the list of things named by Paul in the verses that follow. If one is to continue to argue against baptism in this manner, to be consistent he cannot hold that "call" means to pray in Romans 10:13.

Acts of faith on man's part do not mean that man earns what he receives from God as a result of obedience to something that God himself has commanded. Faith will not save until it works (Jas. 2:14). Faith without works is dead (Jas. 2:26). One is not saved by faith only (Jas. 2:24). The very purpose of gospel preaching is "unto obedience of faith" (Rom. 1:5). If "call" in Acts 2:21 and Romans 10:13 meant to pray, then one would not be saved until he had prayed, which is an overt act. If one *act* of faith (prayer) following a person's initial belief in Jesus Christ is permissible without it being a meritorious act, why would not another overt act of faith (baptism) be valid without it being a meritorious act?

To "call" is *to make an appeal* (cf. Paul's statement, "I *appeal* unto Caesar" in Acts 25:11—the same Greek word rendered "call" in Acts 2:21 and Rom. 10:13 is rendered "appeal" here). When one responds in faith to God through the avenues God Himself has appointed as conditions of salvation, he is *appealing* unto the Lord through his obedience to those conditions for the salvation which the Lord promises upon meeting those conditions. Saul was told to "arise, and be baptized, and wash away thy sins, calling on the name of the Lord" (Acts 22:16). In baptism there is an appeal made to God, there is a calling on, or depending on the Lord in His revealed character and work. As a matter of fact,

every act performed in faith in becoming a Christian, whether it be repentance, confession, or baptism, is an appeal, a calling on, depending on, the Lord to perform according to His promise in giving one the salvation he/she is seeking.

> I do not ask
> That crowds so throng the temple
> That standing room be at a price;
> I only ask that as I voice the message,
> They may see Christ.
>
> I do not ask
> For churchly pomp or pageant,
> Or music such as wealth alone can buy;
> I only pray that as I voice the message,
> He may be nigh.
>
> I do not ask
> That man may sound my praises,
> Or headlines spread my name abroad;
> I only pray that as I voice the message,
> Hearts may find God.

QUESTIONS FOR JOY AND PROFIT

1. In what sense are all men the sons of God?
2. What does it mean for man to be an accountable creature before God?
3. On what basis were the Gentiles accountable to God in the Old Testament period?

4. In what special sense is God represented as Father in Scripture?
5. Will God hear a sinner when he prays? What kind of sinner?
6. What is the meaning of John 9:31? Is a Christian a sinner in this sense?
7. What is the meaning of the words, "Abba, Father"?
8. What prompts the Christian to utter these words according to Gal. 4:5-6 and Rom. 8:15?
9. What does it mean that Cornelius' prayer went up as a memorial before God? Did God hear his prayer?
10. Was Cornelius saved by prayer? What did he need to receive from Peter?
11. What two things are necessary before one can be saved?
12. What is involved in obeying the gospel?
13. Are there any cases in the New Testament where sins were remitted through prayer and repentance? Involving the Christian or non-Christian?
14. Does the statement that the publican was justified mean that he was saved by prayer?

15. Was the thief on the cross saved by prayer? May one be saved like the thief today?
16. When were the terms of pardon in the name of Christ preached for the first time? What were they? Did they include prayer?
17. What had to happen before the New Covenant, represented as a will, could come into effect?
18. What point does Paul make about our relation to the law and to Christ by comparing it to the marriage relationship?
19. When was the law abolished? When did the New Covenant come into operation?
20. Does "call on the name of the Lord" refer to prayer in Acts 2:21? Why? What does it mean in this passage?
21. Does "call" in Rom. 10:13 mean pray?
22. How is the one who believes "call" here means pray usually inconsistent in what he believes about this and what he believes about baptism?
23. What is "calling on the name of the Lord" in Acts 22:16?
24. Saul, like Cornelius, was a praying man before he became a Christian (Acts 9:11). Was Saul saved through prayer?

12

Prayer and Confession

The word commonly translated into our English word "confess" in the New Testament has several varieties of meaning. It sometimes means no more than to concede or allow something. John the Baptist "confessed, and denied not; and he confessed, I am not the Christ" (Jn. 1:20). In response to the inquiry, "Who art thou?" John conceded that he was not the Christ. Paul and Abraham, and other Old Testament worthies either used or had used of them this word with this same meaning (Acts 24:14; Heb. 11:13).

The most common use of the term is to acknowledge a thing, either that Jesus is the Christ (Matt. 10:32-33; Rom. 10:9-10; 1 Tim. 6:12), or one's sins (1 Jn. 1:9; Jas. 5:16). On the day of judgment Jesus will acknowledge those who have acknowledged Him (Matt. 10:32b; Lk. 12:8b; Rev. 3:5). Sometimes the word is used to refer to the acknowledgement of God in a thankful and worshipful manner, "to praise Him" (Rom. 14:11; 15:9; Heb. 13:15).

SIN - CONFESSION - FORGIVENESS

Sin is a transgression of the law, lawlessness (1 Jn. 3:4). In our study we have already seen the kind of priority the Christian is to give to "the will of God." Sin is an infringement of God's revealed will. Such an infringement makes man guilty before God. Guilt of sin is the reason all the world has been "brought under the judgment of God" (Rom. 3:19).

Sinners are treasuring up for themselves "wrath in the day of wrath and revelation of the righteous judgment of God" (Rom. 2:5). God has charged Jew and Gentile alike "that they are all under sin" (Rom. 3:9), for "all have sinned, and fall short of the glory of God" (Rom. 3:23).

But, thanks be to God for His unspeakable gift. "God commendeth his own love toward us, in that, while we were yet sinners, Christ died for us" (Rom. 5:8). Because we have been justified by His blood, we shall "be saved from the wrath of God through him" (Rom. 5:9). God's plan for saving men through Jesus Christ first began to be made known on the first Pentecost following Jesus' resurrection from the dead (Lk. 24:47; Acts 2:37-38; 3:19; 13:38ff.). Through belief in Jesus Christ and obedience to the gospel terms of salvation men are now made free from sin and the coming wrath of God (Rom. 6:16-18; 2 Thess. 1:7-9; 1 Pet. 4:1 7; Mk. 16:16; Acts 2:37-38). On deliverance "from the wrath to come" see 1 Thess. 1:9-10.

This freedom from sin is no guarantee that those who have been justified through the blood of Christ will sin no more. It is a freedom from the guilt of sin, not a promise that one will not sin again. John says, "If we say that we have no sin, we deceive ourselves ..."(1 Jn. 1:8a), and he is writing to Christians. Again, he says, "My little children, these things write I unto you that ye may not sin, . . . " (1 Jn. 2:1), showing that we may sin after we have been saved. The Christian must face the fact of sin in his life, and he must learn how to cope with it. God has not left us without a way out when we sin. John adds, "And if any man sin, we have an Advocate with the Father, Jesus Christ the righteous: and he is the propitiation for our sins; and not for ours only, but also for the whole world" (1 Jn. 2:1b-2).

We see here that the same provision has been made for the sins of the world and the sins of Christians. It is the blood of Christ. In one sense, then, there is no such thing as two laws of pardon, one for the alien sinner and one for the Christian. All forgiveness is on the basis of the same law, namely, the blood of Christ. This is not to affirm that aliens and Christians are saved on the same terms, but that all are saved from sins on the basis of the same law of God—Christ as the propitiation for all sins.

How is the Christian to cope with his sins? He is to rely on the same blood that cleansed him from sin initially (1 Jn. 1:7). John is more specific however. His answer is, confess them:

"If we confess our sins, he is faithful and righteous to forgive us our sins, and to cleanse us from all unrighteousness" (1 Jn. 1:9).

SECRET - PRIVATE - PUBLIC

The book of Proverbs says, "He that covereth his transgressions shall not prosper; But whoso confesseth and forsaketh them shall obtain mercy" (Prov. 28:13). It is understood that whenever confession of sins is commanded, repentance is necessarily involved. When Simon sinned he was told to repent and pray (Acts 8:22). Sins confessed but not repented of would not be forgiven.

Do you suppose that our failure to make the progress we ought to make in our Christian lives is largely due to our failure to confess our sins as we should? This passage says that we do not prosper when we fail to confess our sins. No Christian can grow as God expects him to grow unless he examines himself and allows God to try him with a view to becoming more like Him who died for him. With the psalmist we must cry, "Search me, O God, and know my heart: try me, and know my thoughts; and see if there be any wicked way in me, and lead me in the way everlasting" (Ps. 139:23-24). It is far better to find our faults and confess them than to attempt to hide them from God and others.

Confession of sins should be made to the one against whom we have sinned. Following this guideline we may classify confession under three headings: *secret confession,* made to God alone; *private confession,* made to the person we have sinned against and to God; *public confession,* made before the whole congregation and to God.

Secret confession is "secret" because the confession is made to God alone and involves sins known only to God. Secret sin (Ps. 90:8) is "that which is veiled in distinction from manifest sins" (Franz Delitzsch). They are to be confessed only to God. Such sins are not secret because God does not know them. God knows all about us, so such confession to God is not to inform Him of that about which He is ignorant, but rather to acknowledge what He already knows about us. There is no need for us to attempt to hide our sins from God. Not only is this not possible, but it is foolish. Sin in all of its forms will one day be made known, "for God will bring every work into judgment, with every hidden thing, whether it be good or whether it be evil" (Eccl. 12:14).

Until we confess our sins to God we ought to be just as miserable as David was before he finally acknowledged his sin to God. "When I kept silence, my bones wasted away through my groanings all the day long. For day and night thy hand was heavy upon me: my moisture was changed as with the drought of summer. I acknowledged my sin unto thee, and mine iniquity did I not hide: I said, I will confess my transgression unto Jehovah; and thou forgavest the iniquity of my sin" (Ps. 32:3-5).

When we sin against others as well as against God, our confession must be made to those we have sinned against, and not to God alone. But even here we must be careful that we make the proper distinction between the two. If a man commits adultery in his heart by looking upon a woman to lust after her (Matt. 5:28), must he make confession to her before God will forgive him? No. This is a *secret sin* known only to God, and it must be confessed to God alone.

Only *private* sins are to be confessed to the parties involved, not secret sins. Jesus speaks of private sins in the Sermon on the Mount when He says, "If therefore thou art offering thy gift at the altar, and there rememberest that thy brother hath ought against thee, leave there thy gift before the altar, and go thy way, first be reconciled to thy brother, and then come and offer thy gift" (Matt. 5:23-24). Notice that the order is, "first go ... ; then come . ." When we have wronged our brother we must first be reconciled to him before our worship will be acceptable to God. In a situation where both have sinned against each other, James shows that the confession ought to be reciprocal, "Confess therefore your faults one to another, that ye may be healed" (Jas. 5:16).

The words "one to another" in the passage in James show that where one has injured another confession is to be made to that party. It is likely that James has in mind a situation where brethren have mutually offended each other, in which case they must confess their sins "one to another." If auricular confession as practiced by some wherein the penitent confesses his sins to the priest with a view to an absolution of sin is taught here, then the priest must confess his sins to the penitent as well! It is mutual confession that James is talking about. Nothing is said of confessing faults to those whom we have not injured at all. The idea that some brethren came up with that we ought to have "prayer cells," where Christians get together, turn the lights down low, hold hands, and confess all their secret sins to each other and pray for each other is a far cry from what James is saying we are to do. The Bible does not teach that we are to confess secret sins to anybody but God.

It is just as easy to carry the practice of public confession too far as it is secret confession. Why should one bring before the whole church all of his secret and private sins? There is no example or command in the New Testament that would require a public confession of secret or private sins. Those who demand that a public confession of sins must include a specific listing of all the secret and private sins of the individual are making a demand the Bible does not make. The safe rule to follow is to always make the confession as public as the sin.

PRAISE - WAIT - CONFESS

The Bible does not prescribe any particular order in which the various phases of our prayers are to be offered to God. Any one prayer may consist of various elements, such as praise, thankfulness, petition, and confession. It would seem more fitting that we begin our prayers, both private and public, with praise to God. The model prayer which Jesus gave to His disciples began with ascriptions of praise to God as Our Father: "our Father who art in heaven, Hallowed be thy name" (Matt. 6:9).

There is something in a name, in spite of the words of William Shakespeare: "What's in a name? that which we call a rose by any other name would smell as sweet." Every attribute that the Bible might reveal about God would be summed up in His name. By saying, "Hallowed be thy name," we are thereby acknowledging God for all that He is, the "I AM BECAUSE I AM" (Ex. 3:14). God is the first cause and one cannot get back of Him. We cannot fully comprehend all that God is, but in praising Him by hallowing His name we are humbled in His presence by acknowledging that we know He is great and we cannot fully know Him (Job 36:26). We know only the outskirts of His ways (Job 26:14), His judgments are unsearchable, and His ways past tracing out (Rom. 11:33). Surely we must first come before God in praise. The prayers and songs of praise from the psalms will help us learn how to praise God in prayer (Ps. chaps. 100, 8, 19:1-6; 33, 46, 65, 145, etc.).

Then there must be waiting upon the Lord. "I will wait upon thy name" (Ps. 52:9). "My soul waiteth upon God" (Ps. 62:1). "My soul waiteth for the Lord more than they that watch for the morning" (Ps. 130:6). "They that wait upon the Lord shall renew their strength" (Is. 40:31). These quotations are from the KJV. For the word "wait" the American Standard Version has such words as "hope" (Ps. 52:9) and "silent" (Ps. 62:1, footnote). The idea is that we must be still and rely upon the strength of the Lord. As true penitents we must expect and long for the salvation of God.

In this frame of mind, having praised God and now longing for the salvation which He alone can bring, we are ready to acknowledge our sins before Him. There must, of course, be true penitence. "If I regard iniquity in my heart, the Lord will not hear me" (Ps. 66:18). There must be complete honesty, allowing the Lord to search me, and know my heart, to try me, and know my thoughts. I must want Him to "see if there be any wicked way in me, and lead me in the way everlasting" (Ps. 139:23-24). Then I must specifically name my sins to God, sins of omission and sins of commission, and call upon Him for mercy and forgiveness.

The value of specifically naming our sins does not lie only in the fact that sins must be specifically confessed in order to be forgiven, but in the fact that it helps me to search myself more carefully with the view of not only finding and confessing my sins, but to remove those sins from my life as well.

This plan for prayer is not, of course, laid out for us in the Bible. It is only suggestive and might prove helpful in our efforts to improve our prayers unto God. After we have fully confessed our sins to God we would surely want to thank Him for all of His goodness, and then petition Him for our needs. Some of the psalms will also help us improve in our prayers of thanksgiving (Ps. chaps. 18, 30, 32, 34, 41, 66, 92, 116, 138, etc.).

> Dear Lord and Father of mankind,
> Forgive our foolish ways;
> Reclothe us in our rightful mind,
> In purer lives Thy service find,
> In deeper reverence, praise.
>
> In simple trust like theirs who heard,
> Beside the Syrian sea,
> The gracious calling of the Lord,
> Let us, like them, without a word,
> Rise up and follow Thee.
>
> Drop thy still dews of quietness,
> Till all our strivings cease;
> Take from our souls the strain and stress,
> And let our ordered lives confess
> The beauty of thy peace. Amen.

QUESTIONS FOR JOY AND PROFIT

1. What is the most common meaning of the word "confess" in the New Testament?
2. Name some examples of how the word is used with this meaning.
3. What does it mean to be guilty before God?
4. What is the meaning of the word "justified"? From what and by what?
5. From what two things is man freed by the blood of Christ?
6. When did God's plan of salvation first begin to be preached?
7. Does the fact that man has been justified by the blood of Christ mean that he will sin no more? Support your answer with Scripture.
8. What provision has God made for the sins of the Christian?
9. What is the meaning of the word propitiation?
10. Are the terms of forgiveness the same for the alien sinner and the Christian?
11. What might be one possible cause of spiritual weakness among God's people?

12. What is a *secret* sin? A *secret* confession?
13. Why would it be foolish to try to hide our sins from God?
14. What kind of emotional condition was David in before he confessed his sin to God?
15. Does Matthew 5:28 speak of private or secret sin? What is the difference?
16. Does Matthew 5:23-24 address the matter of private or secret sin?
17. How does failure to confess sin affect our worship to God?
18. What do the words "one to another" in James 5:16 mean?
19. Does James 5:16 teach the doctrine of auricular confession? What is auricular confession, according to the teaching of some? What does "absolution of sin" mean?
20. Does James 5:16 teach that Christians ought to tell all their secret sins to each other?
21. What kind of sins should be confessed publicly before the whole church?
22. What element of prayer is named first in the model prayer in Matt. 6:9ff?

23. What does it mean to hallow the name of God? How should we praise God in prayer?
24. What does it mean to "wait upon the Lord"?
25. What would you say are the most important elements in confessing our sins to God?
26. Should we name our sins one by one when we make confession to God? Why?

13

Prayer and the Intercession of Christ

Christians find themselves in a world which the Bible says is not their home. "This world is not my home, I'm just a passing thru" are words we often sing, but the truth is it is hard for us to fully realize just how much truth there is in these words. Most of us have to grow into full awareness of this fact. We have to live in the world for a while, see all the sickness, heartache and death, and perhaps even experience some of the hardships ourselves, before we come to see that all that belongs to this world is swiftly passing away (1 Jn. 2:17). This world is full of people who never get beyond the thoughts, ambitions and pleasures of this world, and along with the world and its "wisdom," they "are perishing" (1 Cor. 1:18, ASV footnote).

In this world Christians are called to live a separated life, to be holy, even as God is holy (1 Pet. 1:15-16; cf. 2 Cor. 6:14-18). Others may think it strange that we no longer live the rest of our time "in the flesh to the lusts of men, but to the will of God" (1 Pet. 4:2), and that we do not "run ... with them into the same excess of riot" (1 Pet. 4:4). But, that be as it may, as sojourners and pilgrims in this world (1 Pet. 2:11; Heb. 11:13), we are seeking after a country of our own (Heb. 11:14), "a better country, that is, a heavenly," a "city prepared" for us (Heb. 11:16), "the city which hath the foundations, whose builder and maker is God" (Heb. 11:10).

It is not easy to live in a land of exile, or to "pass the time of our sojourning in fear" (1 Pet. 1:17). The Lord never promised that it would be easy: "In the world," He said to the twelve, "ye have tribulation: but be of good cheer; I have overcome the world" (Jn. 16:33). Victory over the world, that is the challenge he left with them. He has left us with the same challenge (1 Jn. 2:15-17), but he has not left us alone. He has gone through what we are now going through in the world, but

He was not of the world, neither are we. That's all He expects of us—in the world, but not of it; and He has given us an example that we might follow in His steps (1 Pet. 2:21-23). Having Himself "endured the cross, despising shame," He has now "sat down at the right hand of the throne of God" (Heb. 12:3). Because He endured what we must endure, He has not forgotten us. He knows the struggle each of us faces.

Jesus understands our plight because He Himself was man, "made like unto his brethren" (Heb. 2:17). He was tempted in all points like we are tempted, yet without sin (Heb. 2:18; 4:15). His likeness to us and His human experience made Him "able to succor them that are tempted" (Heb. 2:18).

CHRIST'S INTERCESSION ON EARTH

Jesus' understanding of our human predicament comes through clearly in several of His statements to His disciples at crucial moments in their lives, as well as in a couple of His intercessory prayers on their behalf. At the moment of His greatest agony when He "offered up prayers and supplications with strong crying and tears unto him that was able to save him from death"

(Heb. 5:7), He returned to the three disciples whom He had left a short distant behind, only to find them sleeping (Matt. 26:36-46). He said to Peter, "What, could ye not watch with me one hour? Watch and pray, that ye enter not into temptation: the spirit indeed is willing, but the flesh is weak."

He left the three disciples two more times, and again they fell asleep both times. This is a striking illustration of how weak man is in the flesh, and the words of Jesus, "the spirit indeed is willing, but the flesh is weak," show His keen insight into the nature of man. He fully understands our weaknesses and temptations. He also knows the importance of prayer in overcoming temptation, especially when prayer is linked with watchfulness. This insight into man's needs came in a large measure through His having become "one" (sharing a common humanity) with us (Heb. 2:11), and through His own temptations and sufferings.

On one occasion Jesus prayed an intercessory prayer for Peter. "Simon, Simon," Jesus said to him, "behold, Satan asked to have you, that he might sift you as wheat: but I made supplication for thee, that thy faith fail not; and do thou, when once thou hast turned again, establish thy brethren" (Lk. 22:31-32). This statement shows that Jesus clearly understands our struggle; He knows that Satan, our chief adversary, is always going about seeking whom he may devour (1 Pet. 5:8); that we must always be on our guard lest we be overcome; and that prayer is one of our primary weapons for overcoming the devil. It also shows that Jesus has a great interest in our spiritual welfare, and that He intercedes on our behalf.

The most detailed prayer of intercession left for us in the New Testament is the one Jesus prayed immediately following his final discourse with his apostles, recorded in John 17. He first prayed for Himself (vv. 1-5), then for His twelve disciples (vv. 6-19), and for all believers and the world (vv. 20-26). Of all that Jesus prayed for in the intercessory part of this prayer the things that stand out the most are those requests which reveal to us Jesus' clear understanding of the dangers we face, and His total sympathy for us as a people who are in the world but not of it (vv. 11, 14, 16).

The most pressing need is that those who are in the world be "kept ... from the evil one" (v. 15). Jesus clearly understands that to remain in the world (and He does not desire that it be otherwise, v. 15a) involves a struggle if we are to remain apart from it. He does not expect us to make it alone. He prayed that the Father would "keep them from the evil one," and "sanctify them in the truth" (v. 17), that His joy might be made full in them (v. 13b). He prayed that all believers might be one in Him (vv. 20ff.), that the world might know that the Father had sent Him (v. 23).

CHRIST'S INTERCESSION IN HEAVEN

Christ has now "passed through the heavens" into heaven itself to appear before God as our great High Priest (Heb. 4:14). His exaltation to the right hand of God has not in any way limited His ability to provide the needs of the saints. It is just one more reason why He is qualified in every way to meet our needs. Hebrews 7:25 says, "Wherefore also he is able to save to the uttermost them that draw near unto God through him, seeing he ever liveth to make intercession for them." Up to this point in the book of Hebrews the following things have been given as reasons why He qualifies to meet every need of the Christian:

1. Through His death by which He made purification for sins He can draw men to God.
2. By His experiences of temptations and trials He can sympathize with us in our infirmities.
3. By the permanency of His life He can save completely.
4. By His prevailing intercession He can bring blessings and favors of God upon us.

Paul also affirms elsewhere that Christ is now interceding on behalf of His people: "Who shall lay anything to the charge of God's elect? It is God that justifieth; who is he that condemneth? It is Christ Jesus that died, yea rather, that was raised from the dead, who is at the right hand of God, who also maketh intercession for us" (Rom. 8:34-35).

To intercede means to "fall in with," to "meet with in order to converse with freely," as we saw in our first chapter on the meaning of prayer. The idea is to plead with a person, or, as W. E. Vine says, intercession is "seeking the presence and hearing of God on behalf of" a person or thing. It is to make requests concerning others, and on their behalf.

We ought to make mention of a couple of other words that mean the same thing as intercession;

namely, the words Advocate and Comforter. Jesus is called our Advocate in 1 John 2:1. This word, according to Arndt and Gingrich, means "one who appears in another's behalf," "an intercessor, helper." It is the word applied to the Holy Spirit by Jesus and is translated into our English word "Comforter" in John 14:16-17. The word "another" in this passage shows that Jesus is also our Comforter. Paul says that the Holy Spirit is also our intercessor (Rom. 8:26- 27). The same Greek word is used in all of these references, showing that both Christ and the Holy Spirit are involved in the work of pleading our case, appearing in our behalf and comforting us. The fact that Luke tells us that the early Christians walked in the "comfort" of the Holy Spirit (Acts 9:31) shows that the Holy Spirit is our Comforter in some sense today, and that He was not a Comforter to the apostles only.

But how can both Christ and the Holy Spirit be intercessors for us in prayer? Doesn't the Bible say that Christ is the only mediator between God and man (1 Tim. 2:5)? Yes, but the work of mediation and intercession are not exactly the same. A number of years ago Hardeman Nichols reminded us of certain differences between the two:

1. A mediator is one who acts between two parties. The intercessor stands by the side of one to plead his case to another.
2. A mediator belongs to two parties while an intercessor represents one party to another (Gal. 3:20, "a mediator is not a mediator of one"). Jesus was both man and God.
3. A mediator is a sponsor or surety, he must interpose some offering of surety or guarantee. Christ gave Himself (1 Tim. 2:6; Heb. 12:24). Though an intercessor pleads on behalf of another, he is not required to make a surety.
4. A mediator is for enemies, while the intercession of the Holy Spirit is "for the saints" (Rom. 8:27).
5. A mediator must ratify His covenant, which Christ did (Heb. 8:6; 9:15; 12:24). The Holy Spirit intercedes according to the terms of Christ's ratified covenant, "according to the will of God" (Rom. 8:27).

The intercession of the Holy Spirit, according to Paul in Rom. 8:27-28, has been explained in various ways. But the simplest explanation appears to be the best one. The "infirmity" of verse 26 refers to our inability to pray as we ought. The "groanings which cannot be uttered" are the same groanings that were mentioned in verse 23; our groanings within us which result from our not knowing what our need is or how that need ought to be met. The Holy Spirit, however, knows our needs and can make them known to God.

It should be a great encouragement to Christians to know that in times of extremity, when we are experiencing great sufferings (v. 18), and we find it hard to pray, or to find the right words to make known our needs, the Holy Spirit intercedes on our behalf before the Father. He pleads our case for us. God, the great heart searcher, knows the mind of the Spirit, or the content and intent of the intercession that the Holy Spirit is making on our behalf (v. 27).

What a wonderful consultation. Just to think that we have all those on earth who are interceding on our behalf—many intercessors on earth—and two intercessors in heaven, the Holy Spirit and Jesus Christ. Brethren, do not forget to pray. Pray always. Pray without ceasing.

> I thought I needed many things
>   Along life's toilsome way,
> When days were long and heavy cures
>   Left scarcely time to pray,
>
> I thought I needed many things
>   For those I held most dear,
> When they were sad and longed for rest
>   Or change of portion here,

> When it was Thee I needed, Lord,
>   To satisfy my heart.
> To fill my days with rest and peace,
>   And every grace impart.
>
> And those I loved, but needed Thee,
>   Not change of scene or place,
> But faith, just now, through sun or shade
>   Thy loving hand to trace.
>
> Just Thee alone, my blessed Lord,
>   For every time and place;
> Just Thee alone—until we all
>   Shall see Thee face to face.

QUESTIONS FOR JOY AND PROFIT

1. What is the meaning of the words "pilgrim" and "sojourner"? In what sense are Christians pilgrims and sojourners?
2. What is the Christian seeking after?
3. What is to be our manner of life as pilgrims and sojourners?
4. What will people in the world think strange about us when we live a separated life from the world?
5. What is there about the nature of Christ that enables Him to sympathize with us in our human condition? How did Christ's experience help Him sympathize with us?

6. What statement in the book of Matthew shows us Jesus' insight into the nature of man?
7. What prayer did Jesus offer to God for Simon Peter? Was it answered? How? What does this prayer show about Jesus' understanding of us? About His interest in us?
8. Jot down the ones for whom Jesus prayed in the following verses in John 17:

   vv. 1-5:

   vv. 6-19:

   vv. 20-26:

9. Which parts of this prayer show Jesus' understanding and sympathy for us in our human condition?
10. What does it mean to "hold fast our confession" (Heb.4:14)?
11. What does drawing near with boldness to the throne of grace refer to in Heb. 4:16? What is mentioned in verse 15 to encourage us to do this?
12. What does Heb. 7:25 tell us Christ ever lives to do for us?

13. What qualifications has the writer of Hebrews given up to this point in the book to show why Christ can meet our every need?
14. What is the meaning of intercession?
15. What other words in the New Testament mean the same thing as intercession?
16. Is the Holy Spirit our intercessor?
17. What is a mediator? Is the Holy Spirit our mediator? Why?
18. Indicate whether the following statements describe the work of a mediator or an intercessor. Use M for mediator and I for intercessor.
    ___ For the saints
    ___ Ratifies covenant
    ___ Offering of surety
    ___ Acts on terms of covenant
    ___ Stands by the side of one
    ___ Belongs to two parties
    ___ For enemies
    ___ Represents one party to another
    ___ Acts between two parties
    ___ Not required to make surety
19. Do the "groanings which cannot be uttered" refer to the groanings of man

or the Holy Spirit? (Read other sources; different views are held)

20. What is "the mind of the Spirit" in Rom. 8:27? Who is the one who searches the heart? (Again, different views are held)

www.ingramcontent.com/pod-product-compliance
Lightning Source LLC
La Vergne TN
LVHW091530070526
838199LV00001B/5